The Elm and the Expert

The Jean Nicod Lectures
François Recanati, editor

The Elm and the Expert: Mentalese and Its Semantics,
Jerry A. Fodor (1994)

The 1993 Jean Nicod
Lectures

The Elm and the Expert

Mentalese and
Its Semantics

Jerry A. Fodor

A Bradford Book
The MIT Press
Cambridge, Massachusetts
London, England

CNRS Editions will distribute the English-language edition in France,
Belgium, and Switzerland.

This book was set in Palatino by The MIT Press and was printed and bound
in the United States of America.

Library of Congress Cataloging-in-Publication Data

Fodor, Jerry A.
   The elm and the expert: mentalese and its semantics / Jerry A. Fodor.
      p.   cm. —(The Jean Nicod lectures; 1993)
   Includes bibliographical references and index.
   ISBN 0-262-06170-8
   1. Content (Psychology) 2. Intentionalism. 3. Intentionality (Philiosophy)
4. Psycholinguistics. I Title. II. Series.
BF40. F63   1994
128'.2—dc20   94-6403
                                                                        CIP

for Ernie and Francesca Lepore

"... *you'll sing it again, and you'll sing it again, and you'll sing it again until you sing it right!*"

—punch line of an old opera joke

Contents

Series Foreword

The Jean Nicod Lectures are delivered annually in Paris by a leading philosopher of mind or philosophically oriented cognitive scientist. The 1993 inaugural lectures marked the centenary of the birth of the French philosopher and logician Jean Nicod (1893–1931). The lectures are sponsored by the Centre National de la Recherche Scientifique (CNRS) as part of its effort to develop the interdisciplinary field of cognitive science in France. The series hosts the texts of the lectures or the monographs they inspire.

Jacques Bouveresse, President of the Jean Nicod Committee
André Holley, Director of the Cognitive Science Program, CNRS
François Recanati, Secretary of the Jean Nicod Committee and Editor of the Series

Jean Nicod Committee

Mario Borillo

Jean-Pierre Changeux

Claude Debru

Jean-Gabriel Ganascia

Michel Imbert

Pierre Jacob

Jacques Mehler

Philippe de Rouilhan

Dan Sperber

Preface

These four lectures were first presented in the spring of 1993. The first two comprised the Kant Lectures at Stanford University, and all four were given to inaugurate the annual Jean Nicod Lectures on philosophy and cognitive science at the *Centre National de la Recherche Scientifique* in Paris. Lecture 4 includes a revised version of part of a paper called "The Dogma That Didn't Bark," that was first published in *Mind* (Fodor 1991a). The rest of the material is new.

Though the lectures have been substantially rewritten (and rewritten, and rewritten) for this publication, I've retained as much as I could of their original style and format. In particular, I've kept the footnotes and references to a minimum. Since the series purports to tell a story that is continuous and self-contained, the reader is spared an introduction. (I have, however, committed two appendices.)

I've been correspondingly informal about notation; the reader is kindly requested to resolve residual ambiguities as their contexts demand. Where it matters, however, I adopt the following conventions: Single quotes distinguish use from mention; expressions in capital letters name concepts (construed as mental particulars and their types); italic expressions name properties and meanings. So, the concept

RED expresses the property of *being red*, and is in turn expressed by the English word 'red'. "'Red' means *red* in English' is taken to be well-formed; indeed true.

The lectures continue, extend, revise and coordinate lines of research that I've been working on ever since *The Language of Thought* in 1975. (That long ago, was it? "They will say: 'how his hair is growing thin!'") So I can't begin to acknowledge all the students, friends and colleagues I have learned from. But I do want to announce a special obligation to several people whose comments on this manuscript led to substantial additions or revisions. These include Ned Block, Gary Gates, Georges Rey and Karen Neander (who provided generous, extensive, and very helpful criticism of the penultimate draft), David Rosenthal, and Steven Schiffer. I am also grateful to Tyler Burge for several years of arguments, back and forth, about narrow content, individualism and the like. That I now think he was nearer right than I about some of this will emerge in what follows.

Finally, special gratitude to the Philosophy Department at Stanford University and to the CNRS for their invitations to deliver these lectures, for their hospitality and conversation, and for the sheer patience and good will with which they sat through this stuff. It was, for me, more than a great honor; it was great fun.

The Elm and the Expert

1   If Psychological Processes Are Computational, How Can Psychological Laws Be Intentional?

Those of you who enjoy messing around in sailboats—or, what I find is cheaper and dryer, reading about other people messing around in sailboats—will be aware of a literary genre in which the author describes, sometimes in lurid detail, one or other of the things that can go wrong at sea, and then offers soothing advice about how to cope with the kind of crisis he has conjured up. I remember once coming across, and being particularly impressed by, a passage that went about as follows: 'What should you do,' the author asked rhetorically, 'if you are in a situation where there is a strong wind, and a lee shore, and your boat doesn't have an auxiliary engine?' Reply: 'Look, *just stay out of* situations where there's a strong wind and a lee shore and your boat doesn't have an auxiliary engine.' I offer this good council as a sort of epigraph to the text that follows. It may be that I have gotten myself into a philosophical situation about which all that can helpfully be said is that I ought not to have gotten myself into it. What I'll be doing in this course of lectures is trying to convince you—or, at a minimum, to reassure me—that that isn't so.

My philosophical project, over the last twenty years or so, has been to understand the relation between a venerable, old idea borrowed from what philosophers call 'folk psychology', and a trendy new idea borrowed mainly from Alan Turing. The old idea is that mental states are characteristically *intentional*; or at least that those mental states involved in cognition characteristically are. The new idea is that mental processes are characteristically computational. My problem lies in the apparent difficulty of getting these ideas to fit together.

In particular, I seem to have become attached to three theses about meaning and mind, each of which I find attractive and none of which I am prepared to abandon without a struggle, but whose mutual coherence it is, to put it mildly, not difficult to doubt. I am thus forced to the optimistic view that these three doctrines must be mutually compatible, appearances to the contrary not withstanding; things must, in short, be better than they seem. I admit at the outset that things are rarely better than they seem, that they are usually a good deal worse, and that the track record of optimistic philosophers has not been impressive.

Here, in any event, is the agenda: In this first lecture I will sketch my budget of theses. I propose to do so only in barest outline, however, hoping to leave room to adjust the details of each to meet the exigencies that the others impose. As I go along, I will suggest, very briefly, why I find them severally appealing, but I won't launch anything like a full-dress defense. As I say, all three seem to me to be plausible; if they don't seem plausible to you, perhaps you'll be prepared to grant them for the sake of the argument. Having thus made out the walls of the cage I'm in, I propose to spend most of the time in the next two lectures looking for exits. At the end of the series, I'll say how these doctrines about meaning and mind connect with an approach to epistemology that I favor.

1. Explanation

I assume that empirical explanation is typically a matter of subsuming events (states, etc. I'm not going to fuss about ontology except where it matters) in the domain of a science under laws that are articulated in its proprietary theoretical vocabulary. And I assume that the reliable explanatory generalizations of any psychology that we can now foresee will be intentional through and through. If there are no intentional laws, then there are no psychological explanations.

The idea that psychological explanation typically involves law subsumption, and the idea that the laws of psychology are typically intentional, are both tendentious. (For a quite different view of how psychological explanation works see Schiffer 1991.) I cleave to the first because it's hard to doubt that at least *some* psychological regularities are lawlike (for example: that the Moon looks largest when it's on the horizon; that the Muller-Lyre figures are seen as differing in length; that all natural languages contain nouns). If this is right, we're going to need a story about how laws work in psychological explanation, whatever other stories about psychological explanation we may also turn out to need.

As for the intentionality of psychological explanations, I'm aware that there are those—mostly in Southern California, of course—who say that empirical theories that appeal to intentional constructs will (or should) be replaced, eventually, by explanations couched in the nonintentional vocabulary of neuroscience. There is, however, not the slightest reason to suppose that they are right to say this, and I don't. That people (and, surely, other higher organisms) act out of their beliefs and desires, and that, in the course of deciding how to act, they often do a lot of thinking and planning, strikes me as maybe empirical in principle but surely not negotiable in practice.

By definition, an intentional generalization is one that subsumes psychological states by reference to their intentional contents. So, typical intentional generalizations might be of the form: 'If you want to ——— , and you believe that you can't ——— unless you ——— then, ceteris paribus, you will perform an act that is intended to be ——— .' E.g.: If you want *to make an omelette,* and you believe that you can't *make an omelette* unless you *break some eggs,* then, ceteris paribus, you will perform an action that is intended *to be an egg breaking.* (Whether the action actually *succeeds* in being an egg breaking depends, of course, on whether the world cooperates and the egg breaks.)

Notice that the beliefs and desires and actions subsumed by such generalizations are picked out by reference to their contents; to what they are beliefs *that,* desires *for* and intentions *to.* Patently, then, if you propose to take it seriously that psychological explanation is intentional, you had better have a theory of content up your sleeve.

2. Metaphysics

I assume that intentional content reduces (in some way or other, but, please, don't ask just how) to information; this is, I suppose, the most deniable thesis in my bundle.

Here again I'm going to scant the details. But the basic idea is this: The content of a thought depends on its *external* relations; on the way that the thought is related to the world, *not on the way that it is related to other thoughts.* It's useful to have a sort of zeroth order, tinker-toy approximation to such a theory to play with. Let it be that *dog* thoughts are about dogs because they are the kinds of thoughts that dogs can be relied upon to cause. Similarly, mutatis mutandis, for thoughts with other than canine contents.

Those of you who have followed the literature inspired by Fred Dretske's book *Knowledge and the Flow of Information* (1981) will be aware that the business of actually working out this sort of theory gets a little complicated. Nevertheless, I have two kinds of reasons for wanting to endorse it.

2.a

The first is that a serious intentional psychology must presuppose the *naturalizability* of content. Psychologists have no right to assume that there *are* intentional states unless they can provide, or anyhow foresee providing, or anyhow foresee no principled reason why someone couldn't provide, naturalistic sufficient conditions for something to be *in* an intentional state.

I don't think that this is especially a point about intentionality; naturalizability, in this broad sense, is a general constraint upon the ontology of all special (i.e., nonbasic) sciences. It's a methodological consequence of our conviction—contingent, no doubt, but inductively extremely well confirmed—that everything that the sciences talk about is physical. If that is so, then the properties that appear in scientific laws must be ones that it is possible for physical things to have, and there must be an intelligible story to tell about how physical things can have them. Geologists would have no right to assume that there are mountains but that they can provide, or anyhow foresee providing, or anyhow foresee no principled reason why someone couldn't provide, naturalistic sufficient conditions for something physical to *be* a mountain.

Well, as far as I can see, of the various proposals around for a naturalistic account of content, only the informational ones appear to have a prayer of working. So, I'm going to hold onto informational semantics if I can.

2.b

Informational theories are, on the face of them, *atomistic* about content. If all that matters to whether your thought is about dogs is how it is causally connected to dogs, then, prima facie, it would be possible for you to have *dog* thoughts even if you didn't have thoughts about anything else. Contrast the kind of semantics that linguists call structuralist and philosophers call conceptual role theories of meaning. According to these, the content of a thought is metaphysically constituted by its role in a belief system (mutatis mutandis, the meaning of a word is metaphysically constituted by its role in a language or in a Form of Life). My view is that all such theories are inescapably infected with holism and are therefore incompatible with the working assumption that the laws of psychology are intentional. If what you're thinking depends on *all* of what you believe, than nobody ever thinks the same thing twice, and no intentional laws ever get satisfied more than once; which is tantamount to saying that there aren't such laws. That, in a nutshell, is why so many semantic holists end up being semantic eliminativists (cf. Quine, Putnam, Rorty, Churchland and, probably, Wittgenstein, among others). For further discussion, see Fodor and Lepore 1992.

I am aware that atomism too is tendentious; on both sides of the English Channel, semantic holism is perhaps the characteristic philosophical doctrine of our time. But, to repeat, semantic holism must be false because it's incompatible with the laws of psychology being intentional, and some, at least, of the laws of psychology *are* intentional beyond serious dispute. By contrast, although I suppose it's *possible* to graft a holistic semantics onto an informational one, the conjunction is unnatural and breeds monsters. Informational semantics, in its natural state, is atomistic. My view is that its atomism is an argument *for* informational semantics, and should be embraced as such.

A brief terminological aside, mostly for purists: Informational semantics is closely associated, in the philosophical literature, not only with the idea that semantical properties are *externalist*, but also with the idea that they are, as one says, *broad*. Actually these three notions are different in quite important ways: You can have an externalist semantics that isn't informational (though not, I suppose, vice versa); and, although the discussion between 'broad' and 'narrow' semantics is often just about externalism, broad theories generally hold that the basic semantic properties of thoughts are truth and denotation, and that is an issue on which narrow content theories tend to be divided. As I say, these distinctions are important, but, to keep the exposition finite, I propose largely to ignore them in what follows and use the three terms interchangeably. In fact, I'm increasingly inclined to think that semantic theories ought to be externalist *and* informational *and* broad, so I'm in trouble if any of these clash with the other doctrines in my bundle.

3. Computation

I assume that psychological laws are typically implemented by computational processes.

There must be an implementing mechanism for any law of a nonbasic science, and the putative intentional generalizations of psychology are not exceptions. An implementing mechanism is one in virtue of whose operation the satisfaction of a law's antecedent reliably brings about the satisfaction of its consequent. (For convenience, I'll often suppose that laws are statements and that they have the logical form of hypotheticals.) Typically, though not invariably, the mechanisms that implement the laws of a science are specified in the vocabulary of some other, lower-level, science. Thus, it's a law that water freezes if it is suitably cooled. The mechanism that implements this law involves various changes of the molecular structure of water that suitable cooling reliably induces. Or, again, it's a law that lift is generated when an airfoil moves through the atmosphere. The mechanism involves the reduction of air pressure along the upper surface of the airfoil, in accordance with Bernoulli's effect. (Note, in passing, that the implementation of a law may, but need not, bring about a *metaphysically* sufficient condition for its satisfaction; it does so in the first example but not in the second.) The explanatory paradigm of laws and implementing mechanisms is familiar, and I take it to apply in psychology as elsewhere. What is, however, controversial is the suggestion that the immediately implementing mechanisms for intentional laws are *computational*. Classical materialism, by contrast, almost always assumed that they are *biological*.

Computational processes are ones defined over syntactically structured objects; viewed in extension, computations are mappings from symbols to symbols; viewed in intension, they are mappings from symbols under syntactic description to symbols under syntactic description. There is a well-known and, in my opinion, completely convincing argument for viewing the implementation of psychological laws in this way: It is characteristic of the mental processes they govern that they tend to preserve semantic properties like truth. Roughly, if you start out with a true thought, and you proceed to do some thinking, it is very often the case that the thoughts that the thinking leads you to will also be true. This is, in my view, the most important fact we know about minds;[1] no doubt it's why God bothered to give us any. A psychology that can't make sense of such facts as that mental processes are typically truth preserving is ipso facto dead in the water.

Well, as Turing famously pointed out, if you have a device whose operations are transformations of symbols, and whose state changes are driven by the syntactic properties of the symbols that it transforms, it is possible to arrange things so that, in a pretty striking variety of cases, the device reliably transforms true input symbols into output symbols that are also true. I don't know of any other remotely serious proposal for a mechanism that would explain how the processes that implement psychological laws could reliably preserve truth. (For example, the idea that psychological laws are implemented by process of association was, and remains, hopeless in this respect.) So I assume that Turing was right: the mind is a computer of some sort or other.

This emphasis upon the syntactical character of thought suggests a view of cognitive processes in general—including, for example, perception, memory and learning—as occurring in a languagelike medium, a sort of 'language of thought'. This too is a thesis for which I am enthusiastic.

So much, then, for a preliminary survey of the three principles I wish to endorse. We now turn to the vexed question whether they are mutually coherent; in particular to examining one of the lines of argument that suggests that perhaps they aren't.

Let's start by considering the notion of implementation in somewhat closer detail. An implementation theory for the law *Fs cause Gs* answers the question: '*How do Fs cause Gs?*' It does so by specifying a mechanism that the instantiation of F is sufficient to set in motion, the operation of which reliably produces some state of affairs that is sufficient for the instantiation of G. Figure 1.1 gives the general idea. Arrows between X and Y mean something like: 'Xs are reliably causally sufficient conditions for Ys.'

In the sort of case that we're considering, the fact that M_Fs cause M_Gs explains the fact that Fs cause Gs. But, patently, the explanation is an enthymeme; it works *only if we can also explain how being F could be sufficient for being M_F, and how being M_G could be sufficient for being G*. I'll borrow a term from Rob Cummins (who, however, uses it to somewhat different ends, as we'll see presently) and call a theory that purports to answer this sort of question a *property theory*. A way to say why it is problematic whether my three working assumptions are mutually coherent is this: It's unclear how they could all three be true consonant with there being property theories for intentional laws.

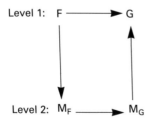

Figure 1.1
Lower-level mechanisms implement higher-level laws. (For simplicity, the diagram assumes that F ⟶ G is not multiply realized.)

Here's the worry. Two kinds of relations between laws and implementing mechanisms are generally recognized by property theories in cases outside psychology, these being *reduction* and *multiple realization*. But, for reasons we're about to consider, the relation between intentional laws and computational mechanisms seems to be of neither of these kinds. So the question arises: what kind of relation could it be?

You get reduction whenever some L-level property P_L is *identifiable* with some L-1-level property. (*Being water* is identical to *being H_2O* according to the usual understanding.) You get multiple realization whenever there is a disjunction of L-1-level properties, such that

i. the instantiation of any of the disjuncts is sufficient for the instantiation of P_L, and

ii. the instantiation of P_L is sufficient for the instantiation of the disjunction but not for the instantiation of any of its disjuncts.

In the classic case of multiple realization, the higher-level property is said to be 'functionally defined', and the realizing disjunction includes all and only the mechanisms that can perform the defining function. (So, for example, there is presumably some disjunction of mechanisms any of which might perform the defining functions of a carburetor, and such that every nomologically possible carburetor is an instance of one of the disjuncts or other.) These days, most philosophers of mind suppose that most psychological properties are multiply realized.[2]

Both the notions of reduction and of multiple realization imply that the instantiation of an L-level property (like F) can be a sufficient condition for the instantiation of an L-1-level property (like M_F), and the instantiation of an L-1-level property (like M_G) can be a sufficient condition for the instantion of a corresponding L-level property (like G). If, for example, F *reduces to* the property M_F, then, of course, every instantiation of the latter is ipso facto an instantiation of the former. Similarly in cases of multiple realization: If, for example, MG_i v MG_j v MG_k . . . etc. is the disjunction that realizes G, then the tokening of any of the disjuncts is sufficient for the tokening of G. It is no accident that both of the concepts typically deployed by property theories should have this feature. As we remarked above, the existence of a mechanism whereby M_Fs cause M_Gs will not explain how Fs cause Gs *unless F is sufficient for M_F and M_G is sufficient for G.*

Let's now consider how these general points about implementation apply to the case we have in hand. If the implementing mechanisms for intentional laws are computational, then we need a property theory that provides for *computationally sufficient conditions* for the instantiation of intentional properties and vice versa. This, however, implies a nasty dilemma.

On the one hand, we've seen that the hypothesis that intentional laws are implemented by computational mechanisms is extremely well motivated; in my view, it's the only account of the semantic coherence of mental processes we have that isn't independently known to be false. But, on the other hand, my assumption 2—that intentional properties are informational and externalist—makes it very hard to see how there *could* be computationally sufficient conditions for their instantiation. How could a process which, like computation, merely *transforms one symbol into another* guarantee the causal relations between symbols and the world upon which, according to assumption 2, the meanings of symbols depend? I can, to return to the tinker-toy example, transform the symbol 'dog' any way I like: I can write the word backwards, or cut off the 'd' or replace it by the word 'cat'. But it is self-evident that no operation of *those* kinds will suffice to connect tokens of 'dog' causally with tokens of instantiated doghood. Or, going in the other direction, how could a causal (or, indeed, any other) connection between 'dog's and dogs guarantee the transformations that a 'dog' symbol may undergo in the course of computational processing? That 'dog's are caused by dogs doesn't prevent me doing anything I like to 'dog' symbols: chopping their 'd's off, writing them backwards, or replacing them by 'cat's, as it might be.

And yet, you can't get computational implementations for intentional laws unless there can be both computationally sufficient conditions for the satisfaction of intentional properties and intentionally sufficient conditions for the satisfaction of computational properties. If this dilemma can't be broken, it looks as though the usual constraints on property theories aren't satisfiable in the case of intentional laws. So maybe intentional properties aren't informational after all; or maybe psychological laws aren't intentional after all; or maybe the implementation of psychological laws isn't computational after all.

It looks like if I insist on assumption 2, I'll have to give up assumption 1 or assumption 3; it looks like I *can't* have both an informational semantics and a computational psychology. Which is irritating, because I particularly wanted to have both.

Here's another way to put the same point. We've seen that, in the (relatively) unproblematic cases, either a higher-level property reduces to its implementing property, or things that have the implementing property thereby satisfy a functional definition of the higher-level property. Now, assumption 3 follows Turing in holding that mental processes are computational; and, as we've seen, it's a point of definition that computational processes are syntactic. That's why computational theories of thinking imply that the medium of mental representation must be languagelike. Well, there's a lot that's dark about syntax, but presumably the following is reliable: If an object (a thought, a sentence or whatever) has a syntactic structure at all, then *what* syntactic structure it has is fixed given just its internal relations; i.e., given its relations to its parts. If, for example, you know what words a sentence is composed of, and what order they come in, you know everything that could be of any use to you in figuring out its syntax; everything, as one says, on which the syntax of the sentence supervenes.

Whereas, by contrast, if externalism is right about semantics, then intentional properties are essentially *extrinsic*; they depend on relations *not between thoughts and their parts, but between thoughts and the world*. But it is, to put it mildly, obscure how a thing could satisfy the conditions for having its *external* relations simply in virtue of having the *internal* relations that it does. It's as though one's having ears should somehow guarantee that one has siblings. But if internal relations don't guarantee external relations, then computational relations don't guarantee intentional relations. Once again it appears that our usual ways of understanding implementation don't apply when the implementee is intentional and the implementer is computational. It looks like something's gotta give.

What gives depends on who you talk to. Searle, Dreyfus, Paul Churchland (when he's feeling connectionist though not when he's feeling eliminativist) and, of all people, Chomsky, want to dispense with the computational level and hold that the immediate implementation of intentional processes is neurological. Stich wants to dispense with intentional laws but hold onto computational explanations. Dennett appears to think that the computational and the intentional are both compounded of stances and loose talk, only neurology being really and truly, stance independently, *there*. And Quine, of course, thinks that *everything* is loose talk except physics and maybe set theory.

In fact, as far as I can see, if the problems about implementation we've been discussing are real and not solvable, only the elimination of the intentional would be a cure adequate to the disease. For, notice: if the externalist character of content shows that the immediate implementation of intentional laws can't be computational, it also shows, and for precisely the same reason, that it can't be neurological (or subatomic, for that matter.) For, neurological states, like computational ones, are individuated by their local properties (roughly, by their relations to their parts and to each other). So, presumably there can't be neurologically sufficient conditions for content states if content properties are externalist. So neurological processes can't implement intentional laws if computational processes can't. So, anyhow, parity with the preceding argument would suggest.

The bottom line seems to be that perhaps there is *nothing* available to immediately implement externalist intentional laws. Here, then, is the full-blown version of my worry: Computational mechanisms implement intentional laws only if computational properties can somehow guarantee intentional ones. But there seems to be no way they could do so on the assumption that the metaphysics of content is informational. And I don't want to give up either the assumption that there are intentional laws, or the assumption that semantic properties are informational, or the assumption that intentional laws are computationally implemented. So, now what?

Property Theories Again

I said that a property theory is anything that purports to account for the relation between implemented properties and implementing mechanisms. This is, however, a slightly eccentric way of viewing them. Compare, for example, Cummins' (1983) treatment: "The characteristic question answered by a property theory is: What is it for system S to have property P? . . . The natural strategy for answering such a question is to construct an analysis of S by appeal to the properties of S's components and their mode of organization. This process often has as a preliminary stage an analysis of P itself into properties of S or S's components"(15). Thus a property theory, in Cummins' sense, is a theory about property *identity*.[3] If you have such a theory, then, as previously remarked, you have no residual problem about how implementing properties could reliably coinstantiate with the properties they implement; if Xs *are* Ys it's transparent why Xs and Ys keep turning up together.[4]

But the question does have to be faced in the present case; if intentional contents are informational and psychological processes are computational, then presumably there won't be a property theory of the Cummins type to relate them. Informational properties can't *be* computational properties since, as we've been seeing, neither is so much as metaphysically sufficient for the other; and, surely, metaphysical sufficiency is the least that property identity requires. So the question arises: What could possibly keep computation and content in phase? To suppose that intentional properties are externalist *and* that Turing was right about how they are implemented seems to imply a sort of preestablished harmony between the intentional and the computational. And for better or worse, preestablished harmonies aren't, these days, in philosophical good repute.

That way of putting the problem does make it sound sort of hopeless. The continuing flirtation that a number of philosophers, myself included, have been having with the notion of 'narrow' content over the last decade or so is, perhaps, best understood in this context. It is obscure how externalist intentional laws could be computationally implemented. Very well, then, let there be *another kind* of intentionality—let there be, as one says, 'narrow' content as well as 'broad' content—such that narrow content is ipso facto *not* externalist. And let it be assumed that the content that figures in psychological laws is, in fact, content of this narrow kind. Then there could after all be computationally sufficient conditions for being in the kind of psychological states that psychological laws apply to—viz., for being in narrow intentional states—and everything is fine.

But, of course, if intentional laws are narrow, then my metaphysical assumption that content reduces to information can't be true. I used to think that the problem of constructing property theories to connect intentional laws with their computational implementations simply *demands* that intentional laws be construed as narrow. But I am now inclined to think that it doesn't and that a purely informational semantics can be reconciled with a purely computational theory of mental processes after all. How to do this, and what it is likely to cost to do it, will be a main theme of these lectures.

A place to start, it seems to me, is to rethink the idea that property theories have to be identity theories. No doubt, general methodological considerations demand that the coinstantiation of implementer and implementee be *reliable and explicable*. But couldn't we perhaps tell a story that would make content properties broad and make the coinstantiation of content properties and computational properties reliable and explicable all the same? Here's a nice analogy (suggested to me by Andrew Milne, a graduate student at Rutgers). Consider the two properties *being a dollar bill* and *being dollar-looking* (by stipulation, a thing is dollar-looking iff it's green, made of the familiar kind of paper, has a picture of George Washington on one side . . . etc; i.e., 'dollar-looking' is stipulated to be rigid). There are, I suppose, reliable, counterfactual supporting generalizations about things that are dollar bills. For example, that were you to offer to swap them one for one for nickels, you would surely get many takers. These generalizations, though reliable and counterfactual supporting, are, of course, nonbasic and hence require implementation.

That is where the dollar-lookingness of dollar bills comes into the story: Generalizations that implicate dollar bills as such are typically implemented by processes that implicate dollar-lookingness as such. Since, as we've seen, implementation requires reliable coinstantiation between implementer and implementee, you might expect that the property of being a dollar and the property of being dollar-looking would generally keep pretty close company. As, of course, they do. It is near enough to being true as makes no matter that all dollar bills are dollar-looking, and that only dollar bills are. *But what maintains them in this correlation?* That question couldn't arise, of course, if *being a dollar* and *being dollar-looking* were the same property, but clearly they aren't. Being a dollar is an extrinsic (causal/historical) property; whether a thing has it depends essentially upon its etiology. Being dollar-looking, by contrast, is a matter of a thing's *internal* properties (it's a property of a thing's *appearance*, whatever, exactly, that may mean). Being dollar-looking isn't even metaphysically sufficient for being a dollar since a thing's appearance may be so contrived as to obscure its etiology; it's here precisely that the forger inserts his wedge. It is also for this reason that the Treasury Department might coherently undertake to make and distribute red dollar bills; dollarhood survives the flux of appearances if the relevant features of etiology aren't disturbed.

Dollar-lookingness reliably coinstantiates with dollarhood; and that they do so is a condition for the one to implement the other. This is unmysterious because, though the properties are not identical, there is a mechanism that functions to keep them in phase. The mechanism, in case you were wondering, is the intervention of the cops. If you attempt to produce (at least in any substantial numbers) objects which are dollar-looking but lack dollarhood, the cops will attempt to prevent you. There are, in principle, many ways that they can do so. For example, they might be able to convince you to desist by bringing it to your attention that the maxim of a forger's act cannot coherently be willed as universal. More likely what they will do is hit you, repeatedly and painfully, with a nightstick which they carry for that purpose. So it is that the coinstantiation of dollarhood and dollar-lookingness, though merely contingent, is nonetheless reliably and explicably maintained. Which, as we have seen, is all that the logic of the implementation relation actually requires.

I pause to emphasize a feature of the example that's especially germane to our purposes. The intervention of the cops provides the mechanism that explains how dollar-lookingness and dollarhood manage to stay linked. Notice that, in the nature of the case, this explanation is *synchronic*: It

invokes a mechanism that operates (or is disposed to operate) *now*. This is as it should be; the correlation of dollar-
lookingness with dollarhood is *currently* reliable, so the
mechanism that sustains it must be *currently* operative. *No
merely historical account will do.*

I am pounding the table about this because, very often,
when I tell people my worry about keeping intentional and
computational properties in phase, what I get for my trouble
is a song and dance about Darwin. "You see," they explain,
"all the creatures whose computational and intentional
properties weren't properly in phase died out long ago."
But no. If you think that's the answer, you haven't understood the question (or you haven't understood Darwin).

No doubt, if there is something in situ that coordinates
the intentional properties of mental states with their computational properties, then some Darwinian process must have
selected it, and its having been selected explains why there
is now so much of it around. But the question before us is
what the mechanism that effects this correlation is, and evolutionary explanations *aren't of the right form* to answer that
kind of question. Evolution maybe explains why there are
more things around that work than there are things that
don't. But it doesn't explain *how* things work, and it is deci-
sively a 'how' question that we're faced with in trying to
reconcile assumptions 1–3. So, please, spare me; no Darwin.

Being a dollar is one thing, being dollar-looking is another; they are distinct but correlated properties, so something
must sustain their correlation. In fact, the cops do. Well,
why shouldn't much the same be true of the correlation
between broad content intentional properties and the computational processes by which they are implemented? No
doubt, it isn't the exercise of police power that keeps these
two in phase; but why, for example, couldn't it just be a law

of nature that they coinstantiate (e.g., why couldn't it just be a law of nature that the M_Gs in figure 1.1 are reliably causally sufficient for the Gs)? This suggestion reverts to a Positivistic conception of scientific architecture, according to which interlevel relations among theories are mediated not by property identities but by (what the Positivists called) 'bridge' laws. Wouldn't that do it in the present case? Wouldn't bridge laws reconcile intentional laws with computational implementations without invoking narrow content?

I shouldn't think so. Assuming that the connection between content and computation is nomic is perfectly reasonable as far it goes, but it doesn't go nearly far enough. Presumably the only basic laws are proper laws of basic physics, and if that is so, then bridge laws that connect content with computation would somehow have to be explained. So postulating such laws doesn't really solve our problem; it only kicks it downstairs.[5] If it's puzzling how broad content laws could be reliably computationally implemented, it's equally puzzling how it could be a law that broad content laws are reliably computationally implemented.

We arrive at crux. It looks as though the best story about meaning we've got—viz., the informational theory—can't be squared with the only story about mind we've got—viz., the computational theory. Not, at least, preserving intelligible relations between psychological laws and their implementing mechanisms. So it looks as though we must either give up on the informational metaphysics of content or we must give up on the computational theory of mind, *or we must somehow contrive to solve this puzzle.* By and large, the philosophical consensus has favored the first or second strategies. In what follows, I propose to explore the third.

We started with an architectural problem about the relation between intentional psychological laws and their presumed computational implementations, but we're now back in territory that is familiar from the philosophy of language. There are, in principle, two kinds of ways in which broad contents and computational implementations might come unstuck. Either many broad contents might correspond to the same computational state (as in Putnam's case of computational Twins with different beliefs); or many computational states might correspond to the same broad content (as in Frege's case, where people who believe that Fa fail to believe Fb, even though a=b).

I assume both kinds of examples are familiar. Frege worries about the man who, despite their identity, believes that The Morning Star is remote but doesn't believe that The Evening Star is remote. Putnam worries about a creature that is molecularly, and a fortiori computationally, identical to me except that he lives in a world where the stuff that looks like water is XYZ rather than H_2O. According to Putnam's intuitions, this creature can't think about water, and can't mean *water* by his utterances of 'water'.

Viewed from the present perspective, Twin cases and Frege cases both suggest that you can't have computational implementations of broad content laws; the reasons they give for suggesting this are different but compatible. Twin cases say that an informational construal of content provides a theoretical vocabulary that is *inadequately abstract* for purposes of psychological explanation. If you insist that computationally implemented intentional laws be externalist, your theory will miss the generalizations in virtue of which my intentional psychology is the same as that of my computationally identical Twin.[6] Frege cases are even worse. They say that if you insist that the belief that Fa is the same as the belief that Fb whenever a=b, the price your theory will pay is *predictive failure*. Fb believers don't, in general, behave like Fa believers whenever a=b, broad content to the contrary notwithstanding. That is precisely because different computational mechanisms implement their (by assumption, content-identical) broad beliefs. Figure 1.2 sketches the situation.

Twin cases show that more than one intentional state (Fl, F2) can correspond to the same implementing mechanism (M1), hence that identity of implementation can't be sufficient for identity of intentional content. Frege cases show that more than one implementing mechanism (M1, M2) can correspond to the same intentional state (F1), hence that identity of intentional state can't be sufficient for identity of implementation. As I say, this is familiar territory: the thought experiments that make the relation between intentional laws and computational implementations problematic are the same ones that are widely supposed to make the relation between sense and reference problematic. It's a

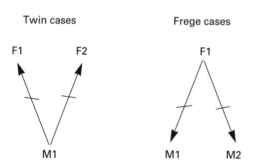

Figure 1.2
Twin cases imply many-one mappings from intentional states to computational implementations. Frege cases imply many-one mappings from computational implementations to intentional states. (⟶|➤ means 'isn't sufficient for'.)

standard view among semanticists that Frege cases show that reference doesn't determine sense and Twin cases show that sense doesn't determine reference.

I would be, to put it mildly, surprised if it turned out just an accident that the worry in semantics about what relates sense to reference and the worry in philosophical psychology about what relates broad (i.e., referential) content to computation have the same geometry. The point of appealing to senses in semantic theories is to provide the extra degree of freedom—the 'mode of presentation' of a referent—that allows extensionally distinct belief states to be type identical and allows type-distinct belief states to be extensionally identical. My guess is that, when all the dust has settled, it will be mental representations—syntactic structures in the Language of Thought—that play this semantical role. But, however that may be, approaching the Frege cases and Twin cases from the perspective of the implementation problems helps one to keep in mind what it is otherwise easy (but disastrous) to forget; namely, that there is a substantial difference between the philosophical question whether our *concept* of content is broad, and the empirical question whether the laws of psychology are laws of broad content.

From this point of view, Frege cases and Twin cases show that content *could* come unstuck from computation; the externalist notion of content is compatible with that possibility. But *it does not follow* that if psychological laws are computationally implemented they must be narrow. All that follows is this: if psychological laws are broad and computationally implemented, then there must be a mechanism whose operation *prevents Twin cases and Frege cases from arising* among creatures that the laws subsume. Or, anyhow, prevents them from arising very often. This is just an application to the present case of the general point that was made above: you don't, strictly speaking, need property *identities* to explain why implementers and implementees coinstantiate; all you need, strictly speaking, is a mechanism that makes their coinstantiation reliable and intelligible.

So here, finally, is the proposal of which the next lecture will scratch the surface: There aren't any narrow contents, and, a fortiori, there aren't any narrow content laws. And there aren't, in Cummins' sense, any property theories for intentional laws. The coinstantiation of broad content with its computational implementers is reliable and explicable but *metaphysically contingent;* that they coinstantiate depends on some very general facts about the world, not on the metaphysical constitution of content as such.

To say that the correlation between computation and broad content is metaphysically contingent is not, of course, to say that it is accidental. I assume that the facts on which it depends obtain not just in the actual world, but in all nearby worlds where the laws of psychology are implemented in the same way that they are here. But if psychological content is broad, then, according to the present view, there are going to be worlds in which metaphysically sufficient conditions for content are satisfied but in which the mechanisms that keep content and computation together in *our* world *don't obtain.* In such worlds, either the bridge laws that relate intentional states to computational processes are *basic;* or intentional laws are *un*implemented (i.e., they are themselves basic); or intentional laws are implemented somehow, but not computationally; or there are intentional states but no intentional laws. What matters, finally, is that the worlds we care about—ours and the nomologically possible ones nearby—aren't of any of these kinds.

So much, then, for a first walk through the problem space. I think there is a crisis brewing in the foundations of cognitive science: There is good reason to think that thinking is computation and that content is information, and yet it's increasingly unclear that the computational theory of mind and the informational theory of meaning can be persuaded to cohabit. These lectures are largely about how to get them to do so.

2   Life without Narrow Content?

The Eponymous Question raised by the first lecture (from here on, I'll call it EQ for short) was how to reconcile the idea that psychological laws are characteristically intentional with the idea that their implementation is characteristically computational. And the main moral of the first lecture was this: If intentional content is broad, then either EQ has no answer, or there must be mechanisms that (contingently) insure that Twin cases and Frege cases don't occur (very often). Since it is surely possible that there should be such mechanisms, the purely philosophical issue may be taken to be settled: intentional laws, externalistically construed, could be computationally implemented if such mechanisms were in place. And, of course, if intentional content is *narrow*, it is unproblematic how intentional laws could be computationally implemented since narrow content supervenes on computational role *by fiat*. Pure philosophy thus reveals two ways in which EQ might have an answer; and, having done so, washes its hands and departs. So like pure philosophy, to leave before the party starts.

An *im*pure philosopher might be curious which, if either, of these ways of answering EQ is the right one. I am an impure philosopher by these standards; perhaps by any.

Metaphilosophical scruples to the wind, I therefore propose to argue, in this lecture, that it is *plausible*—not unreasonable to believe—that the world is so organized as to prohibit the proliferation of Twin cases and Frege cases; hence that, for all we know, the laws of intentional psychology may well be broad. To argue this requires finding something—some mechanism short of a miracle—that might serve to keep broad content and computational role in harmony. What that might be is the burden of what follows.

I pause for emphasis: I'm not going to argue that psychological laws *should* be broadly construed, and I'm not going to argue against narrow content. A fortiori, I'm not going to argue that the notion of narrow content is incoherent or otherwise infirm. What I *am* going to argue is this: the considerations that have been supposed to show that an externalist construal of content won't meet the purposes of psychological explanation are, on balance, unconvincing. So maybe narrow content is *superfluous*.

Harmony without Theology, Part I: Twins and Experts

Twins

Putnam's (1975) story about XYZ shows something about our *concept* of content: it shows that the supervenience of the broadly intentional upon the computational isn't conceptually necessary. But it doesn't argue against the *nomological* supervenience of broad content on computation since, as far as anybody knows, XYZ is nomologically impossible. Almost certainly, chemistry allows nothing that is as much like water as XYZ is supposed to be *except water*. In particular, there are no (nearby)[1] worlds in which

(i) our chemical laws are intact,

(ii) there are creatures whose thoughts are computationally similar to our water-thoughts, but

(iii) these creatures aren't connected to samples of H_2O (either at all or in anything like the way that we are).

If all of that is true, then admitting the conceptual possibility of XYZ is compatible with claiming that *as a matter of nomological necessity* all broad thoughts that are computationally like my water thoughts are content-identical to my water thoughts in all nomologically possible worlds; hence that there couldn't be H_2O/XYZ twins. But if I *couldn't* have a twin, it is no objection to a broad content psychology that if I *did* have one it would fail to express such generalizations as would then subsume us both. Empirical theories are responsible only to generalizations that hold in nomologically possible worlds. (Compare Fodor 1991c, where this rudimentary consideration appears to have been overlooked. The argument there shows that *if there were any twins,* that would preclude an empirical psychology that taxonomizes mental states by their broad content; such a taxonomy would fail to sort things by their causal powers. The hypothetical is well taken, and the considerations Fodor offers in its favor no doubt display a certain low cunning. But since there aren't any twins, who cares?)

So much, then, for XYZ; there isn't any, and there couldn't be any, and so we don't have to worry about it. Unless we've done our science all wrong, it's a moral certainty that the nearby worlds in which our computational psychology holds are a proper subset of the nearby worlds in which our chemistry does.

However, this brusque treatment doesn't generalize; it depends on the nomological impossibility of XYZ, and I suppose it would be foolhardy to claim that Twin cases are nomologically impossible as such. In fact, I don't claim that they are impossible, or even that they don't happen (cf. the familiar story about jade and jadeite). A broad content psychology would fail to express the generalizations that subsume such Twins as there are; and these generalizations the corresponding narrow content psychology could capture. But I claim that though such cases occur, *it is reasonable to treat them as accidents and to regard the missed generalizations as spurious.* For, consider:

1. It's a point of definition that if I am to have a Twin with respect to my concept C, then there must be distinct natural kinds K1, K2 whose instances I do (or would) regularly fail to distinguish when I apply C. ('Do or would regularly fail to apply' means 'do or would fail to apply in the sorts of circumstances which, according to the One True Informational Semantics, determine the broad content of one's thoughts.')

But, of course, that's not enough.

2. It mustn't be that I regularly fail to distinguish K1 and K2 *not only from each other but from all sorts of other things as well;* otherwise C wouldn't *be* a kind concept.

If C is a concept that I (do or would) apply to water and to XYZ but *not* to molasses, or to the sky, or to Colin McGinn, then maybe we have the makings of a Twin case in respect of C. But if C is a concept that I apply not only to water and to XYZ *but also to things belonging to a heterogeneity of other natural kinds,* then, surely, C isn't the concept *of* a natural kind. (Maybe C is the concept THINGS I SAW LAST TUESDAY.) At a minimum, an informational semantics can't regard C as a natural-kind concept since it takes the content of one's concepts to be constituted by one's dispositions to apply them. And informational semantics is being assumed for purposes of this discussion.

3. It can't be a law that the kinds among whose instances I regularly fail to distinguish when I apply C are *very generally* indistinguishable in respect of their causal properties. For, if they were, they would constitute a *functional* higher-level kind, and it would be reasonable to say that C is the concept of that functional kind. Suppose there is some bundle of dispositions D such that, according to The One True Informational Semantics, C applies to Xs just in case I bear D to Xs. Then, for C to be one of my functional concepts *just is* for me to bear D to Xs (not in virtue of the similarity of their microstructures but) *in virtue of the similarity of their effects and causes.*

4. It can't even be a law that K1 and K2 are very generally indistinguishable *in their effects on me*. If they were, then, ceteris paribus, there would be a *subject-relative* functional kind of which K1 tokens and K2 tokens are both instantiations.

Notice that, though they don't have water on Twin-Earth, they do have red and poison and the like. XYZ really is potable, just like H_2O; and twin-roses really are red, just like our-roses. That's because *red, poison* and the like are concepts that things fall under in virtue of their effects on creatures that are physiologically like us; which, by stipulation, includes our Twins. If C is a concept in respect of which I bear D to whatever Xs bear R to me, then, according to informational semantics, C is the concept *of* something that bears R to me.

As far as I can see, given that 1–4 are satisfied, all that's left is that my failure to distinguish K1s from K2s is accidental (even if, at a given place or time, it happens to be pretty general). Perhaps there is somebody else who, also by accident, fails to distinguish K1s from K2s. Then informational semantics leaves it open that his concept might differ in broad content from mine (it's left open that he has the concept of a K1 and I have the concept of a K2). So a broad psychology might miss such generalizations as subsume both him and me. But that's fine since, by assumption, similarities between us that are consequent upon our mutual failure to distinguish K1s from K2s are *accidental*. You don't want a psychology to capture *accidental* generalizations; in fact, you want it to ignore them.

Suppose, for an instance, that there *is* XYZ after all, not just on Twin-Earth but also around here. So the local puddles are sometimes XYZ and sometimes H_2O, depending on which it happens to have been raining. And let it be that, just by sheer luck, all the puddles that you have encountered (a fortiori, all the ones with respect to which you have exercised disposition D) have been puddles of H_2O. Intuition suggests (anyhow, mine does) that in this case C is *not* a kind concept for you, viz., that XYZ and H_2O are both in the extension of your C-beliefs. This is as it should be since, presumably, the One True Informational Semantics will dictate that the dispositions in virtue of which your concept C applies to Xs involve *lawful* (viz., *non*accidental) regularities in your causal interactions with Xs. Correspondingly, a broad psychology will fail to capture the generalizations under which your behavior falls together with the behavior of bona fide water-believers. But this is as it should be too; it is, by assumption, just an accident that you behave like a water-believer (viz., that you apply C to H_2O and not to XYZ). *Failures to capture accidental generalizations don't impugn theories.*

The long and short is this: According to informational semantics, if it's *necessary* that a creature can't distinguish Xs from Ys, it follows that the creature can't have a concept that applies to Xs but not to Ys. Since informational semantics always assigns disjunctive contents in such cases, it never permits twins to arise in respect of them. Informational semantics does, however, allow you to have a concept of Xs even though you don't distinguish Xs from Ys *when your failure to distinguish them is accidental;* i.e., when there's no law that says you can't distinguish them. If, in such a case, you have a twin who also accidentally fails to distinguish Xs from Ys, but whose concept applies to Ys and not to Xs, then a broad content theory would miss a psychological generalization that subsumes the two of you, viz., that you both apply C to both Xs and Ys. But its missing this generalization argues in favor of the theory since, by assumption, it's accidental that the generalization holds.

So far, so good.

Experts

But so far isn't far enough; there is another kind of case (also due to Putnam) in which a diversity of broad contents can correspond to the same implementing mechanism. And, unlike Twins, this kind of case really does proliferate systematically and unaccidentally.

I can't discriminate elms from beeches, but I know that there are experts who can; and, according to the standard story, it's not *my* discriminative capacity but that of the expert that determines the truth conditions of my thoughts about beeches and elms. ELM and BEECH are thus *deferential* concepts for me (though not, of course, for the experts I defer to); so too, mutatis mutandis, for the *words* "elm" and "beech" in my idiolect.

In consequence, when I think *elm* I am in a computational state that is, to all intents and purposes, functionally indistinguishable from the one I'm in when I think *beech*. (The concepts do, of course, differ in the roles they play relative to my dispositions towards utterances of the *words* 'elm' and 'beech'. But familiar considerations suggest that the individuation of the concepts can't turn on this; if it did, monolingual French speakers couldn't think *elm*. For discussion, see Putnam 1975.) Broad content individuation insists, however, on distinguishing between these states since they have, by assumption, different truth conditions. So, here as with Twins, broad content individuation misses generalizations that narrow content individuation can express; broad individuation just can't think why what it takes to be thoughts with quite different contents should nevertheless eventuate in what appear to be identical behaviors. The more of my concepts are deferential, the more of this sort of trouble a broad intentional psychology is going to have. And, as remarked above, though there really couldn't be many Twins, there really could be (indeed there really are) lots of deferential concepts.

The usual philosophical description of deferential concepts is, however, badly confused; when the confusion is dissipated, the existence of such concepts is seen to be of some interest for epistemology but of none for semantics. So I claim.

"I can't tell elms from beeches, so I defer to the experts." Compare: "I can't tell acids from bases, so I defer to the litmus paper"; or "I can't tell Tuesdays from Wednesdays, so I defer to the calendar." These three ways of putting the case are, I think, equally loopy, and for much the same reason. As a matter of fact, I *can* tell acids from bases; *I use the litmus test to do so.* And I can tell elms from beeches too. The way I do it is, I consult a botanist.

What I do with the litmus, and with the botanist, is this: I construct environments in which their respective states are reliable indicators of the acidity of the sample and the elmicity of the tree; in the one case, I dip the litmus into the fluid, in the other case, I point the expert at the tree. I construct these environments with malice aforethought; with the intention that what color the litmus turns (mutatis mutandis, what the botanist says about the tree) will cause me to have true beliefs about whether the sample is an acid (mutatis mutandis, whether the tree is an elm). In effect, I contrive to replace the problem of determining whether the sample is an acid with the (de facto easier) problem of determining whether the litmus turns red. Likewise, mutatis mutandis, I contrive to replace the problem of determining whether the tree is an elm with the (de facto easier) problem of determining whether the expert calls it one.

From the point of view of an informational semantics, the situation is *absolutely normal*: that my *elm* and *acid* thoughts have the content that they do depends on there being mechanisms that reliably correlate them with instantiations of elmhood and acidhood respectively. Epistemologically, however, the situation is remarkable. For one thing, when I use the litmus paper to get my *acid* thoughts correlated with acids, I thereby make the character of the correspondence between my thoughts and the world *a matter of policy*. Only a creature that is capable of *having* policies with respect to its thoughts can do this sort of thing; in all likelihood, we are the only such creatures.

The epistemology of the elm case is still more striking since what I use to manipulate the correlation between my *elm* thoughts and elms is not an instrument but a botanist. To do *that* sort of thing, I must be able to pursue policies with respect to another person's mind as well as my own. And also with respect to the causal relations between our minds. I am relying on its being reliable that elms will cause the botanist to have *elm* thoughts; which in turn will cause him to utter elm reports; which in turn will cause me to believe that it is an elm that I have to do with. Setting things up so that this all *is* reliable requires that I be very clever, that I know a lot (for example, I have to know which experts I can trust) and that I be prepared to pay what a botanist's services cost. But it is likely to be worth the trouble. The correlation between elms and the botanist's *elm* thoughts was hard earned; think of all the dreary years he must have spent in graduate school learning to be a reliable elm-detector. Whereas I can now correlate *my* thoughts with elms practically instantaneously: *My mind-world correlation co-opts his*, much as, in the other case, the correlation between my *acid* thoughts and acids co-opts the correlation between acidity and the color of litmus. What philosophers call 'linguistic deference' is actually *the use of experts as instruments*;[2] not Marxist division of labor in semantics but capitalist exploitation in epistemology.

It is, of course, one thing that I *can* tell elms from beeches (by using an expert); it's another thing whether I actually bother to do so. In fact, for most of my purposes, I don't really care whether a thing is an elm or a beech; the success of most of my elm/beech-directed behavior doesn't depend on my distinguishing between them. (Similarly with acids and bases, so long as the samples are dilute.) The result is that, most of the time, my *elm* thoughts and my *beech* thoughts are indeed identical in their computational implementation and hence in their consequences for my behavior. *Not*, however, because I have the same (narrowly individuated) concept of *elm* that I have of *beech*, but because I am usually indifferent whether I think of a thing as an elm, a beech or, for that matter, as just some tree. Most of the time, *I simply don't give a damn* whether it's an elm or a beech; so, to that extent, I don't give a damn whether my (broadly individuated) thought that it's an elm is true. When I do give a damn, I hire expert help.

Semantics, according to the informational view, is mostly about counterfactuals; what counts for the identity of my concepts is not what I *do* distinguish but what I *could* distinguish if I cared to (inter alia, what I could distinguish by exploiting instruments and experts). Epistemology, by contrast, is mostly about money; e.g., about what I'm prepared to pay to insure that one or other of my beliefs is true, and whether the insurance I can get is worth the cost of the coverage. The usual account of deferential concepts confuses epistemology with semantics, thereby obscuring both; as does, in one way or other, most of what's been written since philosophy took the "linguistic turn." (Previously, modern philosophy had consisted mostly of confusing epistemology with metaphysics. Six of one, half a dozen of the other, as far as I can see.)

One last remark before we change the topic. Having gotten so far, it is now extremely tempting to ask exactly what, according to this account of deference, one's concept of an elm *is*. This question looks to be embarrassing since, as remarked above, familiar considerations suggest that it's not the concept of something that the local experts utter "elm" when pointed at. Posed with this question, the right thing for an externalist to do is, take the Fifth; refuse to answer as a matter of principle. After all, what's being asked is really *what do you have to believe; what inferences do you have to accept* in order to have the (deferential) concept ELM. And it is of the essence of semantic externalism that there is *nothing that you have to believe, there are no inferences that you have to accept,* to have the concept ELM. According to externalism, having the concept ELM is having (or being disposed to have) thoughts that are causally (or nomologically) connected, in a certain way, to instantiated elmhood. Punkt. It is, to put the point starkly, the heart of externalism that *semantics isn't part of psychology*. The content of your thoughts (/utterances), unlike, for example, the syntax of your thoughts (/utterances), does not supervene on your mental processes. There are a lot of people who hold it against externalism that it makes semantics not a part of psychology; and maybe they are right to do so. My present brief is not, however, to reconcile you to externalism. It is rather just to convince you that psychological processes could be computational even if externalism is true and intentional laws are therefore broad.

So much, then, for deferential concepts and for Twins. To construct a Twin case that really would embarrass referential construals of mental content, you would have to show that:

It is nomologically possible that there are creatures for which it is nomologically *im*possible to distinguish between *a*s and *b*s, but of which an externalist theory of content is required to say that they have the concept A but don't have the concept B.

The mental states of such creatures, though 'broadly' distinct by assumption, would be 'narrowly' identical by nomological necessity. A fortiori, a purely broad psychology couldn't articulate the intentional laws that they fall under.

But water/XYZ twins aren't examples of such creatures, because they aren't nomologically possible. And jade/jadeite twins aren't examples of such creatures, because their failure to distinguish jade from jadeite is only accidental. And beech/elm twins aren't examples of such creatures, because they are able to distinguish beeches from elms (by using experts). In fact, as far as I know, there are *no* examples of such creatures. So there's nothing to worry about.

Except the Frege cases.

Harmony without Theology, Part II: The Frege Cases

The Frege cases are the hard ones; so hard, in fact, that one specially interesting variant will have the third lecture all to itself. For the present, I'll be content if I can convince you that there *might* be a reasonable story about why few Frege cases can arise; or, more precisely, why few can arise in ways that would lead to predictive/explanatory failures of broad content psychological theories. It would help me a lot to do so if you would bear it in mind that the issue is *not* whether there are *conceivable* Frege cases; it's not in dispute that there are plenty of *those*. The issue is whether, if intentional laws were couched broadly, the *actual* Frege cases would be plentiful enough, and systematic enough, to disconfirm them.

Intentional psychology is a special (i.e., nonbasic) science, so its laws are ceteris paribus laws. And *ceteris paribus laws tolerate exceptions,* so long as the exceptions are unsystematic. *Exceptions* don't disconfirm ceteris paribus laws though, of course, counterexamples do. So the question whether intentional laws are broad turns *not* on whether there *might* be Frege cases, or even on whether there *are* Frege cases. The sole issue is whether such Frege cases as there turn out to be should be treated as the consequences of failures of ceteris paribus clauses to be satisfied. This issue is empirical, not conceptual. In this context, merely occasional and fortuitous Frege cases don't count; and Frege cases that are merely conceivable don't warrant consideration.

To begin, then: It's true by stipulation that 'Smith believes Fa' and 'a=b' doesn't entail 'Smith believes Fb' if intentional content is supposed to be narrow. Prima facie this is an advantage of the narrow construal; it allows Smith's attitude to Fa to be one thing and his attitude to Fb to be quite another, as indeed they seem to be in the familiar problem cases. (Smith believes that The Morning Star is wet but doesn't believe that The Evening Star is wet, and so forth.) However: Even on the narrow view of content, if the fact is that a=b, then, in the cases that the predictive adequacy of intentional generalizations depend on, *it had better be true reliably, nonaccidentally, and pretty generally, that Smith believes Fa iff Smith believes Fb*. Much of what narrow content gains with its right hand it is therefore forced to return with its left. Here's why:

I assume that any intentional psychology that we can imagine taking seriously will construe a creature's behavior as largely determined by causal interactions between its beliefs and its utilities. My point is that *no* such belief/desire psychology, *broad or narrow,* can tolerate a general proliferation of Frege cases. *Any* intentional psychology, broad or narrow, has to take for granted that identicals are generally de facto intersubstitutable in belief/desire contexts *for those beliefs and desires that one acts on.* For if this isn't granted, there is nothing to connect the rationality of an action with the likelihood of its success. Suppose Fa is something that Smith wants and Fb is something that he doesn't want. Then Smith will find that Fa tastes of ashes if a=b. This is all right as far as it goes; such things happen. Getting what you want can be awful. The problem, however, is that if a=b and Smith doesn't know it, even perfectly prudent behavior in respect of *a* (viz., of *b*) won't tend towards the satisfaction of Smith's desires *except by accident.* And, surely, no serious belief/desire psychology could treat the routine success of prudent behavior as *accidental.*

Smith wants to go to Chicago, and Chicago is where Air Tedium flies to. Unless Smith knows about and acts on this identity, *there's no reason why his wanting to go to Chicago should get him there*; if it does get him there, that's just blind luck. But it couldn't be that the reason people who want to get to Chicago generally do get to Chicago is just that they're lucky. Could it?

Rational behavior is, generally, pretty successful as a matter of fact; a lot more successful, anyhow, than behavior that is simply crazy. No remotely acceptable intentional psychology could count this fact as accidental. But it *would* be accidental—it looks like it would be *unintelligible*—unless, generally speaking, people know and respect the facts that the outcomes of their actions depend upon; including, in particular, the facts about what's identical to what. The *only* means that a belief/desire psychology *has* to insure that, in typical situations where a=b, Smith will assign appreciably similar utilities to Fa and Fb, is to insure that Smith *believes* that a=b and that he makes the relevant inferences.

Short form: Broad content can't distinguish between beliefs (/desires) constructed from denotationally equivalent concepts; narrow content can. But even narrow content explanations have to assume that denotationally equivalent attitudes are generally causally (hence computationally) equivalent in cases where their denotational equivalence matters to behavioral success. Narrow *or* broad, then, every intentional psychology has to posit mechanisms which insure that Frege cases are the exception and not the rule.

I have, from time to time, tried out on philosophical friends this claim that, pretty generally, Smith can be relied upon to know that a=b if the fact that a=b is germane to the success of his behavior. Their reaction has been, I regret to report, strikingly univocal: 'That's much too strong' they say, their eyes wide with incredulity. To the contrary, however; it's actually much too weak. The relevant generalization is something more like this: Agents are normally in *epistemic equilibrium* in respect of the facts on which they act. Having *all* the relevant information—having all the information that God has—would not normally cause an agent to act otherwise than as he does. I'll call this the Principle of Informational Equilibrium (PIE). That Frege cases do not proliferate is among PIE's immediate consequences.

That any belief/desire psychology, broad or narrow, must endorse PIE follows from two truisms:

T1: You cannot choose A over B unless you believe you would prefer A to B if all the facts were known to you.[3] (Notice that rationality would *not* be served by the weaker requirement that you *not* believe that there *are* facts which, if known to you, would reverse your preference. If an agent has no views about what he would prefer if all the facts were in, then if he is forced to choose, the rational thing for him to do is flip a coin.)

T2: The success of an action is accidental unless the beliefs that the agent acts on are true.

From T1 and T2, together with the consideration that no belief/desire psychology can view the normal success of rational actions as accidental, it follows that no belief/desire psychology can fail to accept PIE. Patently, if your belief that you would prefer A over B if all the facts were in is true, then having all the facts wouldn't alter your preference for A over B.

But if belief/desire psychologies are ipso facto committed to PIE, it follows further that, broad or narrow, they are all committed to treating Frege cases as aberrations. This sort of consideration seems to have been widely ignored in philosophical discussions of the significance of Frege cases for the possibility of a broad intentional psychology. Ever since Frege, when philosophers think about the relations between content and action, *Oedipus* is the sort of plot that comes to mind. Oedipus didn't want to marry his mother, but he married his mother all the same. So, it appears, specifications of the contents of Oedipus' attitudes had better distinguish *wanting to marry Jocasta* from *wanting to marry Mother*. So the intentional laws by which O's behavior was subsumed mustn't be laws of *broad* content. Thus a standard argument for the role of narrow content in psychological explanation; thus too, mutatis mutandis, a standard argument for a semantics of sense instead of (or as well as) a semantics of reference.

This is, I suppose, one of the most influential lines of thought in modern philosophy of mind;[4] maybe it's right and we ought, in the long run, to stick with it. But I'm less persuaded than I used to be. Let's try rethinking the case.

Oedipus: The Standard Diagnosis

One might be well advised to bear in mind that in Oedipus' case *something went badly wrong*. In typical examples, when one behaves as one intends, what one gets is what one wants. Oedipus behaved as he intended—he married the lady he meant to; compare the quite different sort of mix-up in *Measure for Measure*, where the wrong girl gets bedded— but, notoriously, Oedipus didn't get what he wanted all the same. Something went badly wrong. *Prima facie, it is a bad idea to take a case where things go badly wrong as a paradigm for cases where they don't.*

What went wrong? Well it seems that Oedipus is an exception to the reliable intentional generalization (reliable in our culture anyhow) that people try not to marry their mothers. Since Frege, the received wisdom has been that Oedipus shows that there's something wrong with this generalization; what we have to do is somehow *fix* the generalization so that Oedipus won't be a counterexample to the revised formulation. Fixing it requires, however, some heavy-duty semantic equipment, and there's not a lot of agreement about how, exactly, the revision ought to go. Among the familiar proposals: *People try to avoid marrying their mothers 'under that description'*; or *people try to avoid marrying their mothers 'as such'*; or *people narrowly-try to avoid marrying their mothers*. It's not clear whether any such account can actually succeed. What people want isn't just to avoid marrying their mothers 'so described'; what they want is to avoid marrying their mothers *at all*. So, at least, one might have thought.

And, of course, to fix the generalization in any of those ways is to give up on reading psychological generalizations broadly; which is how, at least for the sake of the argument, I am trying to read them.

Oedipus Rx

Here is a different prescription: *Don't fix the generalization, fix Oedipus*. There is, according to this revisionist proposal, a true and reliable broad intentional generalization: people try to avoid marrying their mothers. Full stop. Oedipus' case was an exception to this generalization; he did try to marry his mother. Well, you expect reliable generalizations to have occasional exceptions except, maybe, in basic physics. In psychology, as in any other empirical enterprise, the task when confronted with an exception to a generalization that you can usually rely on is to try to show that the case is unsystematic. This strategy seems entirely appropriate in the present case. What happened to Oedipus was exceptional enough to write a play about. Ceteris paribus, good theories want to treat exceptional cases as, well, exceptions.

Can we explain why the generalization that people try not to marry their mothers failed in O's case? Sure; but it takes a lot of machinery. Sophocles, who was no slouch, needs fifteen hundred lines or so of exposition to make the story sound remotely plausible. In the course of which he invokes, inter alia: an abandoned infant who is obligingly rescued by an itinerate shepherd with an inconveniently long memory; a hungry sphinx who likes word games; several proleptic prophecies; two plagues, both of supernatural origin; and an adventitious but fatal highway collision between a father and son, neither of whom manages to recognize the other, though both had been amply warned to stay away from three-way intersections. Also, nobody seems to have noticed what "the ankles of [Oedipus's] feet might witness," viz., "a dread brand of shame that [he] took from [his] cradle. . . . Such that from that fortune thou was called by the name which still is thine." I mean, really; talk about willing the suspension of disbelief!

This stuff makes fine theater all right; my point is that it's also not bad philosophy of science. Circumstances that eventuate in an exception to a generalization that holds ceteris paribus *ought* to turn out to be pretty complicated; by assumption, the generalization would have held if the case had been straightforward. Hard cases make bad laws; only a philosopher would consider taking Oedipus as a model for a normal, unproblematic relation between an action and the maxim of the act. Keep your eye firmly fixed on this: *Most people do* not *marry their mothers*; that, surely, should define the norm.

It matters *very much* in empirical theory construction which cases you take to be the exceptions. My story is that Oedipus is an exception to a generally reliable broad intentional generalization, and that the exception was unsystematic. It's not on the cards that the sort of things that happened to Oedipus could happen in the general case. Rational agents reliably make a point of knowing the facts that the success of their behavior depends upon; we've been seeing that their doing so is a condition for rational behavior to be successful other than by accident. Oedipus, however, failed to find out that Jocasta was his mother, though the fact that she was mattered to the success of his behavior quite a lot. Oedipus was rash and he was unlucky. Because he was rash, he tried to do a thing which, all else equal, he would surely have tried to avoid doing. Because he was unlucky, he succeeded.

Rational acts advance utilities reliably; rash acts advance utilities either by accident or not at all. Rational acts succeed because they have the maxims that they do; rash acts, if they succeed, do so *in spite* of their maxims; which is to say, by luck. The moral of the Oedipus story isn't that intentional laws are narrow; it's just that if you are going to be rash you had better be lucky.

Once again, so far so good. But on reflection this way of telling the story may seem merely to beg Frege's problem. It's one question whether psychological laws are broad. It's a *further* question whether broad content is the only kind that psychological explanations require. If content is construed broadly, knowing that J=J (which O surely did) *is* knowing that J=M (which my version, like Frege's, assumes that he didn't). So, even if one might contrive to hold onto broad psychological *laws* in face of Oedipus' case, doesn't a notion of content that's not broad have to come into the story *somewhere or other?* In particular, don't we have to acknowledge narrow psychological states when we explain why a broad intentional law that is reliable ceteris paribus sometimes *fails?*

Maybe not. Though doubtless O acted out of his beliefs and desires, it does not follow that he acted out of the *contents* of his beliefs and desires. No doubt O wanted to marry J and didn't want to marry M; and, no doubt, explaining what happened depends on distinguishing between these wants. But that the wants have to be distinguished does not entail that their contents have to be distinct.

It's been pretty widely supposed, in discussions like the one that we've been having, that propositional attitudes are, au fond, two place relations; viz., between a creature and a proposition.[5] By contrast, my story is going to be that propositional attitudes are really *three* place relations; viz., between a creature, a proposition, and a mode of presentation. According to this view, Oedipus' desire to marry Jocasta had, as its content, a (broadly individuated) proposition which may be described, indifferently, as the proposition *that O marries J* or as the proposition *that O marries M.* But though the desire to marry J has, ipso facto, the same content as the desire to marry M, and hence falls under the same intentional laws, it does not follow that they are the same desire. In fact, they aren't; they differ in their modes of presentation.

 Propositional attitudes are relations between creatures, propositions and modes of presentation. None of the three is dispensable if a propositional attitude is to be specified uniquely. That's because modes of presentation are sentences (of Mentalese), and sentences are individuated not just by their propositional content but also by their syntax. The identity of their content does not make wanting to marry M the same desire as wanting to marry J, any more than their synonymy makes "John is a bachelor" the same *sentence* as "John is an unmarried man."

What I would really like, at this point, would be for you to leap from your chair uttering wild cries of "Of course, of course; now why didn't I think of that!" But I don't suppose you will. There are, as everybody knows, brutal problems with getting this sort of proposal to work in detail. The third lecture will investigate one aspect of these brutal problems. What I propose to do for now is just summarize the interim morals, handle one objection that's too familiar to ignore, and then finish with an overview.

The Interim Morals

1. If intentional laws are broad and Frege cases are allowed to proliferate, then psychological theories won't be predictively adequate. So anybody who takes intentional laws to be broad must assume some mechanism that operates to block the proliferation of such cases. However:

2. If intentional laws are narrow and Frege cases are allowed to proliferate, then the fact that rational behavior is generally successful is unintelligible. So *both broad and narrow* psychology must assume that Frege cases do not proliferate, and that it's no accident that they don't.

3. That Frege cases don't proliferate is, in fact, a reasonable assumption. 'Intentional systems' invariably incorporate mechanisms which insure that they generally know the facts upon which the success of their behavior depends. That, I suppose, is what perception and cognition are *for*. They operate to insure (inter alia) that stories like *Oedipus* don't constitute the norm.

4. But if it is nonaccidental that Frege cases don't proliferate, then the fact that if they *did* proliferate they *would* disconfirm broad psychological laws is not an argument against psychological laws being broad.

The polemical situation with respect to the Frege cases is not, therefore, interestingly different from the polemical situation with respect to Twins. The conceptual possibility of Twin cases and Frege cases shows that intentional laws *might* not be broad; and the systematic proliferation of either would show that they aren't. But as things stand, neither Twins nor Frege cases offers a convincing argument for narrow content.

5. Frege cases aren't systematic. But they are unlike Twin cases in that lots of them do actually occur. They can't, then, be merely dismissed; they have to be *explained away.* The Oedipus case is typical in that the explanation of an exception to a broad content generalization depends essentially on distinguishing between coextensive attitudes. Oedipus shows that *if intentional contents are broad, then something other than content must be able to distinguish between propositional attitudes.* So be it; propositional attitudes are different if they differ in their modes of presentation. Modes of presentation (have I mentioned this?) are (Mentalese) sentences; sentences are different if they differ in their syntax.

We're almost finished, but I do want to anticipate a line of objection that might be brought against this sort of story *however* the details are handled. It's a well-known worry about *narrow* content that it tends to be a little suicidal. In particular, suppose one's answer to EQ is that narrow content can be implemented by computational role because it is *metaphysically constituted* by computational role. You then face the objection that it is the computational roles of mental states, and *not* their content, that are doing all the work in psychological explanation. Computational role itself is independently motivated; Turing has made it plausible that thought just *is* computation. *Broad* content is also independently motivated because, whether or not it's useful for explaining behavior, we need it to make sense of the fact that thoughts have the truth conditions that they do. But, by assumption, narrow content supervenes on computational role, so what do we need *it* for? Isn't it really implicit in the narrow content picture that the explanation of behavior isn't intentional after all?

This is, in effect, the line of thought that Steven Stich made familiar in *From Folk Psychology to Cognitive Science* (1983), and you might reasonably be worried that the account I've been considering invites much the same question. If content is broad, then behavior is only determined by content taken *together with modes of presentation*. But if Turing was right about psychological processes being exhaustively syntax driven, it looks, once again, as though *content* per se drops out of psychological explanations. It seems that it's the syntactical properties of modes of presentation that are doing all the work, and the attachment to an *intentional*, as oppposed to computational, level of psychological explanation is merely sentimental.

I don't, however, think that this sort of objection works. I think it's possible to imagine a state of affairs in which psychological laws that apply to a mental state *just in virtue of its broad content* might play an essential role in behavioral explanation, even if it is assumed that the *implementation* of psychological laws is sensitive solely to modes of presentation. Let's consider how this might be so.

Suppose that you represent *a* as F (but not as G) and I represent *a* as G (but not as F), where Fa and Ga are, as a matter of fact, both true. We have it by assumption that people generally know the facts that the success of their behavior depends on, hence that such cases won't occur (often) when the price of representing *a* as F and not as G (or vice versa) is behavioral failure. But what about when that's *not* the price? Suppose that I often think of water under the mode of presentation 'Granny's favorite drink' and suppose that you, not knowing Granny, don't. This sort of thing must happen all the time, and it can be perfectly innocuous. There's no reason why it should get you into trouble that you don't know that Granny likes water best; and there is also no reason why our water-directed behaviors shouldn't very largely overlap despite this presumed difference in our collateral information.

We might, indeed, imagine the following, vaguely Wittgensteinian, situation: there is a whole population of creatures (and/or of time slices of the same creature), any pair of whose modes of presentation of water overlap partially, and also differ partially, in much the way that I'm supposing that yours and mine do; but who nevertheless form a natural domain for psychological explanation because the conditions for successful water-directed behavior are fairly uniform in the ecology that the creatures occupy, and because each has beliefs about water sufficient for the reliable success of its water-directed actions. Question: Under what description would the laws of psychology subsume this population? Not, in the circumstances described, by reference to their modes of presenting water; there need be no sentence of Mentalese that all—or even very many— of them reliably have in their heads whenever they think, as it might be, that water quenches thirst. Perhaps, then, only such *broad and intentional* descriptions as, for example, 'creatures which think that water quenches thirst' will serve to pick the population out. Maybe the only thing that can reliably be said about populations whose minds all have modes of presentation of water, but do not all have *the same* modes of presentation of water, *is that water is what they all have modes of presentation of.* I do not say that, qua creatures with *water* beliefs, you and I and our friends and relations constitute such a population. But I don't see any principled reason why we couldn't, consonant both with mental processes being exclusively syntactic *and* with there being robust and indispensable generalizations about the behavior of *water*-believers as such.

It may be that *P-believer* can pick out a psychological natural kind when 'P' is broadly construed; and it may be that (barring open disjunctions of modes of presentation) it's the *only* description that can. Suppose, for example, that some sort of causal account of broad content is correct. Then all *water*-believers must have modes of presentation that trace back, in the right way, to interactions with water. My point is that, qua *water*-believers, they needn't have *anything else* in common: Their shared causal connection to water has left its mark on each of them—they all have modes of presentation of water—but it hasn't left the *same* mark on each of them—their modes of presentation of water differ in lots of ways. Couldn't *water*-believers nevertheless be reliably enough alike in their water-directed behaviors to make them a natural kind for purposes of psychological explanation? If not, why not?

One can, I think, imagine a world where everything is delicately balanced in the following way: Content is broad, the metaphysics of content is externalist (e.g., causal/informational), and modes of presentation are sentences of Mentalese. Modes of presentation with similar causal histories (or nomic affiliations; anyhow with similar broad contents) overlap enough in their syntax to sustain robust psychological generalizations. But not enough to make the minds that these generalizations subsume homogeneous under *syntactic* description. Both the similarities and the differences among the modes of presentation of water would be explicable: On the one hand, the heterogeneity of individual experience accounts for differences of collateral information; on the other hand, we are all much the same sorts of creatures, and we are all causally connected to the world in much the same sorts of ways. No wonder if, de facto, minds that all exhibit the impress of a connection to water do so in ways that regularly overlap. In such a world, the laws that a computational psychology implements might be *intractably and ineliminably* intentional precisely *because* they are laws about *broad* content; viz., laws about a kind of content that computationally heterogeneous minds can share in virtue of similarities in their *extrinsic* relations. Maybe *our* world is like that; whether it is, is *strictly* an empirical issue.

The picture I'm painting is sort of Leibnizian: Qua P-believers, we are all monads (only with our windows open) mirroring the fact that P. 'Mirroring the fact that P' is something like: being in states that are caused by, and hence bear information about, the fact that P. These information-bearing states are syntactically structured, and their syntax drives our behavior, just as Turing said. It's a fact about the world that the causal properties of our minds are pretty similar, and that the causal chains that connect our minds to the fact that P aren't *arbitrarily* various. In consequence, the syntax of the mental representations which have the fact that P in their causal histories tends to overlap in ways that support robust behavioral similarities among P-believers. The world thus sustains a harmony between the (extrinsic/historical) properties in virtue of which a Mentalese sentence is a mode of presentation of the proposition *that P* and the (intrinsic/syntactic) properties in virtue of which a

Mentalese sentence is reliably a cause of the sorts of behavioral proclivities that the laws of psychology say that P-believers share. The harmony thus established between broad content and computational role, though contingent, is reliable enough to answer EQ: computational-syntactic processes can implement broad-intentional ones because the world, and all the other worlds that are nomologically nearby, arranges things so that *the syntactic structure of a mode of presentation reliably carries information about its causal history.* Just as the cops so arrange things that dollar-lookingness reliably carries information about dollarhood.

I've simplified for exposition, so this picture needs retouching (for example, I prefer a nomic-informational story about the metaphysics of broad content to a causal-informational one.) But I think that it will serve for purpose of orientation. I must say, I find it sort of amusing: It would be a really lovely irony and, in light of the views I've previously professed, a great joke on me, if it turned out to be not the narrow but the broad kind of content that makes psychology both irreducibly intentional *and* irreducibly computational.

3

Rabbit Redux (or, 'Reference Scrutinized')[1]

The second lecture in this series closed with a tentative proposal about the individuation of thoughts: Having a thought is being in a three place relation between a thinker, a (broad) content, and a mode of presentation. Since modes of presentation are linguistic expressions (e.g., sentences of Mentalese) and since linguistic expressions are individuated (inter alia) by their syntax, token thoughts are type distinct if they differ *either* in their contents *or* in their modes of presentation.

This treatment of the individuation of thoughts is, of course, tailor-made to mediate between a semantics that wants to reduce meaning to information, and a psychology that wants to reduce thinking to computing. On the one hand, the informational theory says that content is constituted by symbol-world relations. It is therefore hard put to see how *Jocasta* thoughts could differ in content from thoughts about O's M; or, to vary the example, how thoughts about water could differ in content from thoughts about H_2O.[2] On the other hand, computational psychology requires syntactic differences between *water* thoughts and H_2O thoughts *whether or not* they are identical in content. This is because they have different causal powers, and, according to the

Turing picture of psychological processes, the causal powers of mental states supervene on their syntax.

So, then, if thoughts with identical contents may nevertheless be distinguished by their syntax, semantics gets a solution to the Frege problems that's compatible with its externalism, and psychology gets a solution to the Frege problems that's compatible with its computationalism, and both have cause to rejoice. Suppose it turns out that *the very same* syntactic structures that semantics needs mental representations to have in order to accommodate the Frege cases will also serve to define the domains of computational mental processes. That would show beyond any serious doubt that Turing and Dretske between them have solved the mind/body problem. The foundations of cognitive science would then be secure, and the philosophy of mind would have nothing left to worry about. (Except consciousness.)

This all seems rather promising, but of course it isn't free. According to the present treatment, lots of what are intuitively differences between the *contents* of thoughts turn out to be *syntactic* differences between thoughts of the same content. It turns out, for example, that 'H_2O' and 'water' are synonyms and that 'water is H_2O' is analytic, i.e., true in virtue of meaning (though not, of course, knowable a priori). To think that water is wet or that H_2O is wet is thus to think the same propositional content, albeit having the thoughts is being in different mental states. Pretheoretic intuition, not having considered the possibility that thoughts might differ otherwise than in their contents, is, no doubt, affronted. Myself, I don't know how much weight pretheoretic intuition can bear in such cases; content, synonymy, analyticity and the like are, after all, technical notions. If *all* that's wrong with a theory is that it affronts intuitions, perhaps the thing to do is get the intuitions fixed.

Anyhow, here's a soothing thought: if you can't get a *semantic* difference between the concept WATER and the concept H_2O, you can perhaps get the next best thing: despite their synonymy, the conditions for *having* the concepts are different. You can have H_2O only if you have the concepts H[YDROGEN], 2 and O[XYGEN]; but having the concept WATER requires none of this. (You can't have H_2O without H, because H is a syntactic constituent of H_2O; and concepts, since they are linguistic entities, have their constituent structures essentially.)

As I say, this all seems sort of promising; but we're about to have serious trouble. According to the suggested analysis, 'H_2O' and 'water' carry the same information and are therefore synonymous. The familiar examples of failures of substitutivity in contexts like 'has the concept . . . ' are explained by assuming that *content* identity is necessary but not sufficient for *concept* identity. This idea works—if it does—because, although Frege cases show that concepts that carry the same information are not always the same concept, at least Frege cases are compatible with a semantic constraint on concept identity that I'll call condition C:

C: *Concepts that carry the same information are always coextensive.*

J and O'S M are true of the same woman, and WATER and H_2O are true of the same stuff, so C survives both cases.

Suppose, however, that C were to prove unreliable. Then we could no longer pursue the strategy of claiming that informationally equivalent concepts are ipso facto semantically equivalent, and appealing to syntax to explain away apparent counterexamples. Since *semantically equivalent expressions must apply to the same things,* the reliability of C is a necessary condition for the reduction of content to information. If C fails, pure informational semantics fails too.

We are about to consider some examples where C does fail; you get informationally equivalent expressions which *don't* apply to the same things and therefore can't be synonyms. These examples are worrying in a way that mere Frege cases aren't. Frege cases suggest that informational semantics is insufficiently refined to be the whole story about conceptual identity, but they are quite compatible with conceptual identity being a *conservative extension* of informational identity. For all that the Frege cases show, 'carries the same information as' distinguishes fewer things than 'is the same concept as' (it's less 'fine grained'), but at least the latter respects all of the distinctions that the former draws. By contrast with the Frege cases, examples where C fails suggest that taxonomy by informational identity and taxonomy by extensional identity *cross-classify* the concepts. As far as I can tell, they imply that the theory of content can't be either purely informational or purely atomistic. Concessions will have to be made.

I'll argue, however, that the concessions that have to be made are harmless. Although informational semantics isn't strictly true, what's wrong with it doesn't threaten either Realism or Naturalism about meaning. And it doesn't invite Meaning Holism either.

Quine's Puzzle

How do we know that 'rabbit' refers to rabbits and not to *undetached proper parts* of rabbits (hereinafter urps)? Conversely, how do we know that 'undetached proper rabbit part' (hereinafter 'urp') refers to urps and not to rabbits? Call this question Q (for Quine and for convenience). I propose to answer Q presently, but some preliminary comments are required. These follow in no particular order.

1. For present purposes it's convenient not to distinguish the question whether 'rabbit' is *referentially* indeterminate between rabbits and urps from the question whether it is indeterminate between *meaning rabbit* and meaning *urp*. In effect, wherever it doesn't matter, I shall speak as though meaning determines reference; in particular, as though synonymous expressions are ipso facto referentially identical. I would be surprised if the argument proved to depend on this.

2. Q is about *content* individuation, not (just) *concept* individuation: 'rabbit' and 'urp' can't be synonyms because they aren't even coextensive; in fact, anything that either applies to thereby fails to satisfy the other. So, (mere) syntax won't answer Q; we can't, for example, exploit the fact that 'part' occurs in 'urp' in the way that we were able to exploit the fact that 'H' occurs in 'H$_2$O'. 'Water'/'H$_2$O' is arguably (just) a grain problem; 'rabbit'/'urp' is a cross-classification problem.

From this perspective, the examples of putative referential inscrutability that one finds in the philosophical literature are a mixed lot. Though no rabbit is an urp, I suppose that every rabbit is and must be an instantiation of rabbithood, and that nothing else can be. That is, 'rabbit' and 'instantiation of rabbithood' are necessarily coextensive. Because they are, the question why 'rabbit' doesn't mean *instantiation of rabbithood* is not crucial for an informational semantics in the way that, according to the present analysis, the question why 'rabbit' doesn't mean *urp* most certainly is. It would, for example, be open to an informational semantics to hold that 'rabbit' *is* synonymous with 'instantiation of rabbithood', the difference between them being not in what they mean but in the concepts they express.

3. Q looks to be an epistemological question, and the philo-sophical literature often takes it that way. But I don't. The question I propose to answer is metaphysical and *not* episte-mological. It's something like: *What, if anything, makes it the case* that 'rabbit' refers to rabbits and 'urp' refers to urps? On what, if anything, does this difference in reference super-vene? Epistemological considerations have no status in metaphysical inquiries according to my religious principles.

I stress this because, according to the answer that I'll give, that 'rabbit' means *rabbit* rather than *urp* in Smith's mouth depends, inter alia, on what inferences Smith accepts. And one might wonder *how one would tell* what inferences Smith accepts, given, as it might be, facts about the (e.g., verbal) behaviors that Smith emits. Or how a 'radical translator' or a 'radical interpreter' could tell, consonant with the con-straints that define their epistemic positions. Wonder what you will, of course, but for present purposes I have no inter-est in these questions. I assume that there are facts about what Smith (and others) are prepared to infer from what. I propose to appeal to such facts freely in what follows.

4. 'Rabbit' and 'urp', though not coextensive, are neverthe-less invariably *coinstantiated*; every rabbit has and must have undetached rabbit parts, and every urp must be undetached from some or other rabbit. It is therefore true in this and every other possible world, that a situation is one in which rabbithood is instantiated iff it's one in which urphood is. A fortiori, any event that contains the information that either is instantiated contains the information that the other is instan-tiated too. I conclude that no purely informational semantics can distinguish the meaning of 'rabbit' from the meaning of 'urp'.

I can't prove this, of course; it depends on what one's notion of information is, and who knows what notions of information may still await discovery? But I do think we'd better assume it. In fact, I think we'd better assume that no purely *externalist* semantics can prefer "'rabbit' means *rabbit*' to "'rabbit' means *urp*'. Here's why: Externalist semantics has only two ways to distinguish between expressions for properties that are locally coinstantiated. When they are *not* coextensive it does so by appealing to counterfactuals; in effect, by finding a possible world in which only one of the expressions is satisfied. If all and only the rabbits in our world have rabbit flies, and if 'rabbit' nevertheless means *rabbit* and not *rabbit fly*, then there must be some *other* world where the rabbits come without the flies or the flies come without the rabbits. By contrast, if symbols that are coinstantiated in point of conceptual or metaphysical necessity are also necessarily coextensive ('triangular' v. 'trilateral'; 'water' v. 'H_2O'; 'rabbit' v. 'instantiation of rabbithood'), externalist semantics bites the bullet, assumes that they are synonymous and distinguishes them by their syntax, as previously explained. But though 'rabbit' and 'urp' are *not* coextensive (and hence, a fortiori, are not synonymous), they are nevertheless invariably coinstantiated; there *aren't* any worlds in which one but not the other is satisfied. Pure externalism has, therefore, no resources left to cope with them.

5. I think that Q has an answer, but I'm leaving it open whether every similar question does. That is, I'm leaving it open that there may be *some* referential indeterminacy left over when all the metaphysical facts are in. That it is sometimes indeterminate whether 'x' refers to xs wouldn't entail that there aren't *any* facts about what refers to what; it wouldn't entail that reference isn't real.

It is, for example, perfectly OK for someone who is agnostic about whether it's determinate whether number words denote sets to hold nonetheless that *of course* 'rabbit' denotes rabbits. Correspondingly, that it tolerates indeterminacy is not *per se* an objection to informational (or, indeed, any other) semantics; a theory that is true tolerates whatever there is. Quine's question is embarrassing because it suggests that an informational semantics tolerates indeterminacy *where it seems intuitively obvious that there isn't any*. It seems intuitively obvious that 'rabbit' means *rabbit* and not *urp*, and this seems, prima facie, to be an intuition that informational semantics can't capture. If the intuitions were that the reference of 'rabbit' is indeterminate, then its failure to answer Q would argue *for* an informational theory.

6. I take it that Q is a question about reference *rather than truth*. I take its implication to be that the predicate 'is a rabbit' is indeterminate between meaning *is a rabbit* (hence being satisfied by rabbits) and meaning *is an urp* (hence being satisfied by urps), and that this is so *even if the truth values of all the sentences that contain that predicate are fixed*. Specifically, if Q is unanswerable, then any English sentence of the form 'a is a rabbit' is equally legitimately analyzed as being true iff some individual designated by 'a' is a rabbit, or as being true iff some individual designated by 'a' is an urp. On this reading, Q *grants* the syntactic notions *term of L, sentence of L* and *predicate of L* and suggests that the extensions of its predicates and the reference of its terms are underdetermined by the truth values of L's sentences. Q expresses the intuition that there is something wrong with the semantics of terms and predicates—i.e., with the referential semantics of the syntactic constituents of sentences—even if there is nothing wrong with the idea that sentences *have* syntactic constituents or with the idea that they have determinate truth values.

I will therefore take the syntactic notions *sentence, predicate* and *term* and the semantic notion *truth value* for granted in what follows.

7. I propose to consider Q in the following, austere form. Imagine a game involving two linguists (Ling1 and Ling2) and an informant (Inf) who speaks a language L. For convenience, let L be English, though nothing turns on this. Ling1 says that 'rabbit' means *rabbit*, Ling2 says that it means *urp*. The game consists of their attempts to defend these theses in face of the data that Inf provides. In particular, the linguists are allowed to specify any pair they like of a sentence of L and a possible situation, and Inf will tell them whether he takes the sentence to be true in that situation. Inf is, in effect, the embodiment of a (partial) function from situations and sentences of L to truth values. So, for example, given the data Inf provides, the linguists know that Inf holds 'there's a rabbit' true in a situation iff he holds 'there's an urp' true in that same situation.

I further assume that the linguists are given the semantics of the sentential connectives of L for free. (Remember: the intuition behind Q is that the semantics of *sub*sentential expressions is indeterminate even if the semantics of the sentential expressions is fixed. There is supposed to be a metaphysical problem about reference *over and above* whatever metaphysical problems there may be about truth.)

Finally, in order to make it absolutely clear that the issues about to be discussed aren't epistemic, I assume that the linguists' access to their data is unlimited and that the informant is always *right* about which sentences in his language express truths. In effect, I read Quine as betting that even a linguist who knows which sentences *God* holds true couldn't distinguish an ontology according to which 'is a rabbit' applies to rabbits from an ontology according to which it applies to urps. I'm betting that Quine is wrong to hold this.

OK; here's how the game is played. When Inf judges sentence S to be true in situation N, Ling1 must show that S's being true in N is compatible with 'rabbit' meaning *rabbit* in L. For example, if 'rabbit' is a term in S, then there must be a rabbit in N for it to refer to; if '(is a) rabbit' is the predicate of S, there must be a rabbit in N for it to apply to. And so on. Similarly, mutatis mutandis, Ling2 must show that S's being true in N is compatible with 'rabbit' meaning *urp*.

Here's how the game is scored: To find a datum that Ling1 can cope with and Ling2 can't would be to answer Q, so if there is such a datum, I win. If both linguists can cope with all the data, reference is inscrutable and Quine wins. If Ling1 fails and Ling2 doesn't, then 'rabbit' determinately means *urp*, nobody wins, and it's the end of the world.

I'm about to propose what I take to be a winning strategy for Ling1. I'm going to do this, however, in two trips; first, I'll suggest an answer to Q which, though it looks promising, turns out on inspection not to work. I think the way that it fails is illuminating and justifies the indirection. I'll then say what I take the right answer to Q to be and what morals it has for informational semantics.

First Fling at Q

Here's a gambit Ling1 might try. Suppose, for reductio, that 'is a triangle' means *is an undetached proper part of a triangle* and 'is a square' means *is an undetached proper part of a square*. And now, consider the situation illustrated in figure 3.1, where a square overlaps a triangle at a point A. A is a proper part of a triangle, so Ling2 predicts that Inf accepts 'A is a triangle'; A is a proper part of a square, so Ling2 also predicts that Inf accepts 'A is a square'. But, presumably, here and elsewhere, Inf accepts 'A is a triangle' only if he *rejects* 'A is a square' and he accepts 'A is a square' only if he rejects 'A is a triangle'. This seems to show that either 'is a triangle' doesn't mean *is a part of a triangle* or 'is a square' doesn't mean *is a part of a square*. Or, of course, both. Parallel arguments would show that Inf doesn't mean *urp* by 'rabbit'.[3]

This is, first blush anyhow, an attractive line of argument. After all, *being a square* and *being part of a square* are different properties; if they weren't, we wouldn't be having our present difficulties. Since they are different properties, it's not implausible that there should be some other property P such that

A thing's instantiating P is incompatible with its being a square, but compatible with its being a part of a square.

Being a triangle will do in the present case since, though nothing is both a square and a triangle, some triangles are parts of squares. If Inf's behavior signals that a thing has P,

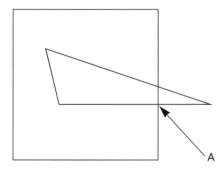

Figure 3.1
A triangle intersects a square at point A. See text.

it *thereby* signals that the thing may be a square part but can't be a square. The rest is duck soup.[4] It seems, at a minimum, that actually *showing* that Inf's ontology is indeterminate between *so and sos* and *such and suches* requires showing that there isn't a property that is situated with respect to *so and soness* and *such and suchness* in the way that being a triangle is situated with respect to being a square and being a part of a square. For all I know, however, there always are such properties; in which case there is no referential indeterminacy.

As I say, this seems, first blush, an attractive line of argument. But, on second thought, it begs the question against Ling2 and Quine. The tactic was to construct a situation in which Ling2 is forced to make a prediction that is contrary to fact—viz., that Inf will accept both 'A is a triangle' and 'A is a square'. That this prediction *is* contrary to fact is supposed to follow from two assumptions: first, that Inf is an informant about English, and second, that Inf accepts only sentences that are true in English. But it does *not* follow from these assumptions. You need also that 'A' unambiguously names A in both sentences; or, if you like, that the individual named by 'A' in 'A is a triangle' is the very same individual that is named by 'A' in 'A is a square'.

Let us pause to recapitulate.

Recapitulation

We could rule it out that 'triangle' means *triangle part* (mutatis mutandis, that 'rabbit' means *urp*) if we could establish that Inf rejects at least one of 'A is a triangle' and 'A is a square' in the situation diagramed by figure 3.1. To show that, we need:

i. Inf is a truth teller

ii. 'A is a square' is true only if 'A is a triangle' is false.

To get ii, however, we need iii *and iv*:

iii. 'is a square' means *is a square* and 'is a triangle' means *is a triangle*.

iv. 'A' unambiguously names A.

We get i–iii by assumption. But where does iv come from?

The moral seems to be something like this: Its being a fact that 'A is a triangle' means *A is a triangle* in Inf's mouth crucially depends on its being a fact that 'A' in Inf's mouth unambiguously names A. But for 'A' to be unambiguously the name of A is, at a minimum, for every token of 'A' *to name the same individual* as every other. So, the most that the first-fling argument could show is that we can rule out Ling2's ontology *if we can determine when two of L's expressions name the same thing.* Perhaps that's progress, but it's surely a good way short of answering Q. An inquiry into the ontology of reference must not presuppose the notion of *co*reference.

We are now well situated to see why it is so natural to despair of answering Q. Let us, therefore, reformulate.

Reformulation

It's untendentious that the data Inf supplies constrain the linguists in the following way:

v. If L takes 'is F' to mean *is F*, then, if there is in situation N an individual which is F according to L's ontology, L must predict that Inf takes 'is F' to be satisfied in N.

Thus, Ling1, who takes 'triangle' to mean *triangle*, must predict that Inf takes 'is a triangle' to be satisfied in figure 3.1; and so too, mutatis mutandis, must Ling2, who takes triangle to mean *triangle part*. But, of course, both 'is a triangle' and 'is a triangle part' *are* satisfied in figure 3.1; so v doesn't suffice to rule out Ling2's deviant ontology.

What *would* do the trick, however, is vi.

vi. If L takes 'is F' to mean *is F* and 'is G' to mean *is G*, then, if there is, in N, an individual which is both F and G according to L's ontology, L must predict that Inf takes 'is F' and 'is G' to be satisfied *by the same individual* in N.

That vi is stronger than v is evident on the face of it; and figure 3.1 shows that vi can't be met on the assumption that 'triangle' means *triangle part*. But we can't enforce vi unless we know *not just which expressions Inf takes to be satisfied, but which expressions he takes to be satisfied by which individuals*. That is, we can't enforce vi unless we already know a lot about how Inf is ontologically committed. So it seems that v is too weak, and vi begs the question. Dilemma.

To break this dilemma, we need some premise which, if granted, would license the inference from 'Inf takes F to be satisfied in N' and 'Inf takes G to be satisfied in N' to 'Inf takes F and G to be satisfied *by the same thing* in N'. The thesis that reference is inscrutable can now be seen as the claim that only question-begging premises could warrant such inferences.

So much for reformulation. We are now in a position to answer Q.

Reference Scrutinized

Suppose we translate 'A is a square' and 'A is a triangle' according to the deviant scheme, *leaving it open* whether the 'A's are coreferential. In effect, we know that what he accepts commits Inf to *some x satisfies 'is a square'* and to *some y satisfies 'is a triangle'*, but we don't know whether he is committed to $x = y$. Is there any further fact about what sentences Inf accepts that could tell us that he is so committed?

Well, yes. If 'A' is an ambiguous name, then 'A is a square' and 'A is a triangle' can both be true in the same situation. *But 'A is a square and a triangle' can't be.* To put it the way linguists do, you can't conjunction reduce across a referential (or other) ambiguity. So, then, if we know that Inf accepts the inference from 'A is F' and 'A is G' to 'A is F and G', we *thereby* know that 'A' is referentially unambiguous in the premises. This isn't a special property of conjunction. Parallel remarks apply if, for example, Inf accepts the inference from 'Neither A is F nor A is G' to 'A is neither F nor G'. Etc.

In English and every other language I've heard about, the semantic function of predicate structures like 'is A (connective) B' is to insure that, when the predicate is evaluated, 'A' and 'B' are applied *to the same individual.* So, for example, if the connective is a conjunction, the predicate is satisfied iff the same individual satisfies all of the conjuncts. Knowing whether Inf accepts an inference from sentential to predicate conjunction thus gives one the same sort of information that one gets from knowing which individuals Inf takes to be identical and/or which names he takes to be unambiguous. So, if we know that Inf accepts the inference from:

(1) 'A is a triangle'

and

(2) 'A is a square'

to

(3) 'A is a square and a triangle'

we don't need further premises to decide whether 'square' means *square part* and 'triangle' means *triangle part.* Inf means *square part* by 'square' and *triangle part* by 'triangle' only if he takes it that 'is a square and a triangle' is satisfied in figure 3.1. But, by assumption, Inf *never* holds 'is a square and a triangle' to be satisfied, either in figure 3.1 or elsewhere[5] So Inf doesn't mean by 'square' and 'triangle' what Ling2 says he does. So far so good.

We now have is what is called in Quinese an 'imminent' (as opposed to a 'transcendent') solution to the problem raised by Q. In effect, we can reject the deviant ontology for a language *in which we can identify such constructions as, e.g., predicate conjunction*. Since we know that 'is ——— and ——— ' is the construction that expresses predicate conjunction in English, we can reject the hypothesis that 'triangle' means *triangle part* in English. That the deviant ontology of L is excluded by determining which sentences with predicate connectives Inf holds true is, I think, not without interest; you might have supposed that it can only be excluded by determining which sentences that express identities Inf holds true. Quine says things about the inscrutability of reference that suggest that he does think this.

We're not, however, out of the woods. Here's the problem. In effect, we have it that if 'is ——— and ——— ' means predicate conjunction in English, then 'is a triangle' doesn't mean *is a triangle part* in English. And, of course, 'is ——— and ——— ' *does* mean predicate conjunction in English, so the argument goes through. Where, however, does the minor premise come from? On what does the fact that 'is ——— and ——— ' means predicate conjunction itself supervene? What we want is that it should supervene *on facts that are fully specified when one says which sentences Inf holds true*. Otherwise it's left open that the intuition that 'is ——— and ——— ' means predicate conjunction is itself a product of such ontological intuitions as that 'rabbit' refers to rabbits and not urps. In which case, appealing to the first intuition in support of the second merely begs the question.

This is, course, a characteristically Quineian style of polemic: You could fix the ontology of English given the intuition that 'same' means *same* since the satisfaction conditions for 'same rabbit' are different from the satisfaction condition for 'same rabbit part'. But whether 'same' means *same* is itself up for grabs unless the ontology of L is determinate. In particular, if Quine is right, it isn't determined by facts about what sentences Inf holds true; viz., by facts of the kind that, by the rules of the game, constitute the linguist's data. And the rules of the game aren't gratuitous. If we were to assume that the linguists know not only what expressions Inf takes to be satisfied but also what he takes them to mean or which individuals he takes to satisfy them, we would be taking for granted precisely the semantic facts whose status we are attempting to determine.

Short form: Q is answered if we can identify predicate conjunction (and the like) in L just on the basis of which sentences in L Inf holds true. Well, can we?

No. But what we can do is just as good for the purposes at hand. We can identify predicate connectives if we know which sentences Inf holds true *and what inferences he is prepared to draw from them.* The details would likely enough be quite complicated, but the basic idea is clear enough: A predicate connective '*' is predicate conjunction if(f?):

Inf always takes sentences of the form 'A is F * G' to imply the corresponding sentence conjunction 'A is F and A is G'; *and*

whenever Inf is prepared to accept 'A is F * G', he is prepared to infer 'A is F * G' from 'A is F and A is G'.[6]

Notice that it is left open that there may be cases where Inf accepts 'A is F and A is G' but is *not* prepared to infer 'A is F * G'. Intuitively, these are the cases where 'A' is ambiguous in the premises (or where 'F' or 'G' is ambiguous between the premises and the conclusion).

The moral, to repeat, is that if you want to know which structures in L are predicate conjunctions, you need to know not just which sentences L-speakers hold true, but also (some things about) which inferences L-speakers are prepared to draw. This should seem unsurprising on reflection since it is entirely plausible that if you want to know which structures in L are *sentence* conjunctions, you also need to know (some things about) which inferences L-speakers are prepared to draw.[7]

A word about inferring, since it has now begun to loom large: The metaphysical context of this entire discussion has been a certain naturalistic framework within which semantic notions are reconstructed in, roughly, causal/nomological terms. In that framework, it's reasonable to assume that inferring is fundamentally a matter of *causal relations among sentence tokens.* In particular, *there is some (probably quite complicated) causal/nomological relation (call it CN) such that Inf infers 'S' from 'P' if(f?) Inf bears CN to (ordered) pairs of tokens of 'S' and 'P'.* No doubt CN will involve not only Inf's actual causal history but also his dispositions with respect to merely possible tokens of the types 'S' and 'P'. So be it.

Many philosophers will find this sort of treatment of inferring tendentious, not to say unbearable. Ah, well. My point is that it's natural for a naturalist to assume it, and that *he does not beg question Q by doing so.* The reason it's un-question-begging is that we have Turing's assurance that inferring is a computational process, hence that CN is a relation that sentence tokens enter into just in virtue of their syntax. We don't have to determine that Inf means *a is F* by 'a is F'—

indeed, we don't have to know *anything* about what Inf means by 'a is F'—to determine that he infers 'a is F' from 'a is G'.

So, then, assuming that inferring is naturalized by invoking CN, we get the following account of predicate conjunction. '*' means predicate conjunction in Inf's mouth if(f?) R:

R:
(i) Inf bears CN to <<'a is F * G'>, <'a is F and a is G'>> whenever he accepts 'a is F * G'. (In effect, Inf is prepared to infer a sentence conjunction whenever he accepts the corresponding predicate conjunction;) and

(ii) If Inf accepts 'a is F * G', then he bears CN to <'a is F and a is G', 'a is F * G'>. (In effect, Inf is prepared to infer any predicate conjunction he accepts from a corresponding sentence conjunction.)[8]

My claim is that R characterizes predicate conjunction in L in terms of sentence conjunction in L, and that it does so *without* assuming that the terms/predicates of L are unambiguous. In particular, R determines predicate conjunction in L relative to a specification of the syntax of its sentences, the truth values that Inf assigns to them, and the inferential cum causal relations among their (actual and possible) tokens. I also claim that this determination is transcendent (it works for any language that has both predicate conjunction and sentence conjunction) and that it does not, in and of itself, beg the question against referential inscrutability.

And, given an un-question-begging characterization of predicate conjunction, we have an answer to Q. For, as we've seen, the facts about which conjoined predicates Inf accepts rule out the ontology according to which 'triangle' means *triangle part* and, mutatis mutandis, they rule out the ontology according to which 'rabbit' means *urp*.

So much for Q. For all Q shows, reference is scrutable after all.

The Cost of Scrutability

Ernie LePore and I used to go around asking philosophers the following sort of question: 'Imagine a language that doesn't have an expression that translates our word 'animal'. Could it have an expression that translates our word 'rabbit'?' (If this question doesn't grab you, try: 'Imagine a mind that hasn't got the concept ANIMAL; could it have the concept RABBIT?') We were interested in such questions because it seemed to us that if the answer is 'no,' then there might well be a slippery slope to the conclusion that no language could translate *any* English expression unless it could translate *every* English expression. For a variety of reasons that we set out in our book *Holism* (1992), this is a conclusion one might well wish to avoid.

To put it in slightly other terms, it seemed to us likely that either translation is an *atomistic* relation, so that what translates an expression of L is independent of what, if any, other expressions L contains; or translation is a *holistic* relation, so that what translates an expression of L depends on *all* the other expressions L contains. We saw no stable middle ground short of wholesale appeals to the analytic/synthetic distinction, which, following Quine, we took to be a Very Frail Reed.

That all this should be so is, after all, exactly what informational semantics predicts. What information 'rabbit' carries depends on whether and in what way 'rabbit'-tokens covary with instantiations of rabbithood. There being such covariation is presumably metaphysically independent of any other symbol-world relations, so information, as such, is purely atomistic. Accordingly, if meaning is information and translation preserves what an expression means, translation should be atomistic too. Pure informational semantics thus entails that whether a language contains an expression that translates the English word 'rabbit' is independent of any *other* facts about its expressive power.

It seems, however, that pure informational semantics is wrong to say this. 'Rabbit' determinately means *rabbit* and determinately doesn't mean *urp*, and the previous discussion suggests that this depends, in fairly intricate ways, on the logico-syntactic apparatus that English makes available to its speakers. I say it *suggests* this. The most it could actually *show* is that the distinction is supported when the apparatus is intact. It's left open that there could be some *other* way for 'rabbit' to determinately mean *rabbit* rather than *urp*; some way that's compatible with semantics being strictly atomistic. I admit, however, to not having a clue what this other way might be, and I am therefore prepared to concede that the cost of 'rabbit''s referential scrutability is that semantics isn't strictly atomistic and hence that it isn't strictly informational.

Never mind. Even if a language that can translate 'rabbit' has to have predicate connectives, it doesn't follow that it has to have an expression that can translate 'animal'. So, even if the metaphysics of referential determinacy shows that semantic atomism is strictly false, it's still wide open that you can say *rabbit* (and/or think RABBIT) even if you can't say (and/or think) *animal*. The reason is that, so far at least, the inferential apparatus that makes 'rabbit' referentially scrutable is exhaustively "logico-syntactic"; we've found no reason to suppose that it infects the *non*-logical vocabulary.

Here's how you run a slippery slope argument for semantic holism. First you get a guy to admit that nothing in a language that can't say *animal* could mean what 'rabbit' does in English. Then you ask about *carrot*; if, after all, meaning *rabbit* depends on accepting the inference from *is a rabbit* to *is an animal*, why doesn't it also depend on accepting the inference from *is a rabbit* to *likes to eat carrots*? What principled difference could make one of these inferences meaning-constitutive and the other not? 'Gee, I don't know,' your interlocutor replies, having read Quine. Holism follows.

My present point is that you can't run this line of argument if there *is* a principled difference between the meaning-constitutive inferences and the rest; and, for all that the metaphysics of scrutability shows, there perfectly well may be. It looks like various pieces of logical syntax have to be in place for Inf to mean *rabbit* rather than *urp*. And, no doubt, terms in the logico-syntactic apparatus are largely *inter*defined. Presumably a language that didn't have 'not' couldn't have 'if', and maybe a language that didn't have sentence conjunction couldn't have predicate conjunction. But there is no reason at all to suppose that the logico-syntactic vocabulary is itself interdefined with the *non*-logical vocabulary. So, even on the assumption that having *rabbit* requires having predicate-*and*, there is no reason to suppose that having *rabbit* or having predicate-*and* requires having *animal*. For all that the metaphysics of scrutability shows, you *can* have *rabbit* without having *animal*; structuralists in linguistics and conceptual role semanticists in philosophy to the contrary notwithstanding.

Semantic atomism is the idea that the meaning of your words—mutatis mutandis, the contents of your thoughts—is metaphysically independent of the inferences you are prepared to draw. In this sense, it's the idea that semantics isn't part of psychology. I think that the puzzles about scrutability show that semantic atomism is probably false in this strong form. The ontology of a language supervenes not on mind/world connections alone, but on mind/world connections *plus logical syntax.* Having said this, however, it's important to add that, for most philosophical purposes, it doesn't matter a damn. It doesn't imply holism about meaning, it doesn't imply that the conditions for a term's meaning what it does are other than well-defined, and what it tells us about naturalism in semantics is only something that we already knew; viz., that the program fails unless there is a naturalistic account of inferring. Since inferences are surely part of the causal structure of the world, this is true *whether or not they are constitutive of meaning.*

Yes, but What Does 'Gavagai' Mean?

Suppose that the distinction between an expression of L meaning *urp* and its meaning *rabbit* depends, metaphysically, on the logical syntax of L. And suppose that the linguistically interesting facts about a certain informant are exhausted by this: He accepts 'Gavagai' when and only when he is visually stimulated by rabbits. (More precisely, when and only when he bears to rabbits, and hence to urps, whatever relation your semantics says is constitutive of carrying information about rabbits, and hence about urps.) What does 'Gavagai' mean in this informant's mouth? Thinking about this question is a way of finding out how far we have, and how far we haven't, departed from a strictly informational semantic theory.

The question has, I think, a perfectly good answer. But I can't tell it to you, and I'm afraid you wouldn't like it if I could. The reason I can't tell it to you is that, to put it very approximately, 'Gavagai' means *gavagai*, and that it does is not something that you can say in English.

Notice, to begin with, that there is no problem about saying what information 'Gavagai' carries in the informant's mouth. Let P be the property that something has iff it instantiates rabbithood[9] or any property that is necessarily coinstantiated with rabbithood. Then Inf's utterances of 'Gavagai' carry the information that P is instantiated; and it's precisely things that instantiate P that the expression applies to in Inf's dialect.

But, of course, 'Gavagai' doesn't *mean* P, assuming that meaning is what translations are supposed to preserve. The trouble is that translation works like indirect quotation and de dicto belief ascription; all three require the preservation not just of content (i.e., information) but also of appropriate relations among modes of presentation. Just which such relations *are* appropriate depends, I think, on the purposes at hand in a given case. For that reason, I doubt that rigorous conditions for translation, indirect quotation or de dicto belief ascription can be formulated (see Fodor 1992).

The problem about translating 'Gavagai' into English is that the only modes of presentation of the property P that English affords are long and disjunctive; and, of course, there is no reason at all to suppose that Inf has anything long and disjunctive in mind when he says 'Gavagai' in the situation we have been imagining. Presumably, what he has in mind is just GAVAGAI.

If, as I've been suggesting, distinguishing rabbits from their undetached parts depends on having access to constructions like predicate conjunction, then speakers of Gavagese can't refer either to rabbits or to their undetached parts; the best they can do is refer to things that instantiate

P. So, we can't translate them, but we can refer to things that they can't. As a matter of fact, I don't suppose there are any languages, or minds, that can express P but don't have predicate connectives and the like. So I don't suppose that there are, as a matter of fact, any languages or minds that can't share our ontological commitments with respect to rabbits and rabbit parts, or whose modes of presentation we can't, at least roughly, approximate in translations. But this is at best a *contingent* truth according to the present account. Nothing about the metaphysics of meaning or of reference guarantees it. In ways that pure informational semantics does not, the mildly mixed view at which we have now arrived tolerates the possibility of minds and languages whose ontological commitments are inscrutable to us and to which our ontology is equally obscure.

Qua speaker of Gavagese, Inf is so situated that he can't mean or refer to what we use 'rabbit' to mean and refer to; and it's true that no purely informational semantics—indeed, no purely atomistic semantics—can account for this. But nothing metaphysically important follows; in particular naturalism about semantics is unimpugned. For all that has been shown so far, the meaning of 'rabbit' is fully determinate, and the conditions for referring to rabbits can be exhaustively and precisely specified in nonintentional and nonsemantic vocabulary. *That we can't translate Inf and Inf can't refer to rabbits does not, therefore, make intentional psychology a philosophically interesting science.*

In which case, who cares whether atomistic semantics is literally true? Not me, I assure you.

4   Why We Are So Clever; An Epistemological Postlude

I started these lectures by rehearsing several assumptions that I'm partial to: that psychological laws are intentional, that semantics is purely informational and that thinking is computation. I've been arguing that, notwithstanding first impressions to the contrary, it is perhaps possible to hold onto all of these assumptions at once, and that the theory of the mind that emerges if one does so is, maybe, one that we could live with.

In this talk, I want to turn from the internal coherence of the theory to some of its foreign affairs. One of the reasons it would be nice to have a respectable philosophy of mind is that one's treatment of other philosophical issues, from metaphysics to epistemology and, no doubt, on beyond to ethics, aesthetics and philosophical anthropology, depends a lot on what one thinks that minds are like. What follows, in no particular order and without the slightest claim to comprehensiveness, are comments on some of these connections with large matters.

Since large matters sort of scare me, this will be rather a short lecture. But I want to say enough to make it plausible that the theory of mind I've been selling you does good work in adjacent fields, and that that is a reason for you to consider buying it. I'll argue, in particular, that the notion that the causation of behavior is mediated by mental representations may be just what's needed to solve one aspect of the mind/body interaction problem; and that the notion that the content of mental representations is constituted by their etiology may be just what's needed to connect computational psychology with naturalized epistemology.

Interaction

The processes that adjust one's behavior to the environment's demands are typically mediated by having thoughts. Thoughts are mind dependent by definition, but they affect things that aren't mental, and are affected by them. *Thoughts are part of the causal structure of the world.* How this could be so isn't the most interesting mind/body problem, but it's one that's starting to look tractable. (The most interesting mind/body problem is how anything material—for that matter, how anything at all—could be conscious. The problem of consciousness, however, does *not* look to be tractable.)

There are, roughly speaking, three kinds of philosophical opinions about how thoughts could interact with things that aren't themselves mind dependent.

• There is the view that the problem doesn't arise, either because, as behaviorists and elminativists say, there aren't any thoughts, or because, as Idealists say, *everything* is mind dependent.

• There is the Cartesian view, which is that the interaction problem does arise but is unsolvable because interaction is miraculous.

• And there is the mental representation story, a version of which I have been trying, in the course of these lectures, to construct.

Behaviorism, eliminativism and Idealism are preposterous on the face of them. They are councils of despair and deserve to be spurned as such. *Of course* behavior is mediated by thinking, and *of course* rocks, trees and the like aren't mind dependent. And I have trouble with the Cartesian view because I don't believe in miracles. That doesn't leave a lot of options for solving the interaction problem.

It is, to repeat, puzzling how thought could mediate between behavior and the world. This puzzle was, I think, misdiagnosed by Wittgenstein, Ryle and a lot of midcentury philosophers whom they influenced. The trouble isn't—anyhow, it isn't *solely*—thinking that thoughts are somehow immaterial. It's rather that thoughts need to be in more places than seems possible if they're to do the job that they're assigned to. They have to be, as it were, 'out there' so that things in the world can interact with them, but they also have to be, as it were, 'in here' so that they can proximally cause behavior. Thoughts need to be both *cognitive* and *executive* if they're to be what makes the structure of behavior responsive to the structure of the world; and, ontology to one side, it's hard to see how anything *could* be both.

It's an old idea, but none the worse for that, that postulating mental representations is the key to solving this puzzle. For, it's of the essence of mental representations that they face two ways at once: They connect with the world by representing it, by and large, veridically; and they connect with behavior by being its typical proximal cause. Because they do both of these at once, they're custom-made to be what mediates the world's behavioral effects.

From this perspective, mental representations seem almost too good to be true; which is, of course, what philosophers who don't like them have against them. For, the question now arises how anything could have the properties that mental representations are alleged to have; in particular, how anything with representational (or semantic, or intentional) properties could be a cause. There does seem to be a certain lack of precedent; prima facie, propositions have semantic properties, but they don't make anything happen; and rocks, trees and the firing of neurons cause things, but they have no content.

The question how mental representations could be both semantic, like propositions, and causal, like rocks, trees and neural firings, is arguably just the interaction problem all over again, so it may appear that mental representations merely recapitulate the problem that they were meant to solve. I think this complaint is inconclusive. But it's quite true that to assume a psychology of mental representations is largely to replace the interaction problem with the representation problem; specifically, with the problem how anything that is ontologically on a par with neural firings can be semantically evaluable. Correspondingly, the motivation for wanting to naturalize mental representation is more than an access of metaphysical scruples. If the representation problem replaces the interaction problem, then the latter is solved if anything could do what mental representations are alleged to do; viz., both cause and represent. The naturalization project is the attempt to show how something can.

That mental states have both representational contents and causal powers is, as I say, not a new idea. For example, Hume had it. (I expect he got it from Descartes and Descartes got it from Aristotle. I don't know who it was that invented it; probably someone who lived in a cave.) What makes our mental representation theory seem more hopeful than Hume's is that we have accounts of representation and of the proximal causation of behavior which seem independently promising, and which, if the arguments in these lectures are right, mesh with one another.

Hume seems to have thought that mental representation is iconic and that mental causation is associative, hence that the interaction problem would be solved if there are mental images whose causal relations obey associative laws. Pictures, because they are symbols, are exactly the right sorts of things to have both representational and causal properties; prima facie symbols are the *only* things other than thoughts that do. Hence the appeal of trying for a single theory of representation that covers both.

As it turned out, however, Hume's solution wasn't worth what it cost. Though he had a story about how ideas could be both causal and representational, Hume had no story about *how what ideas represent and what they cause could be coherently related.* Associations, after all, are supposed to depend on the *statistics* of thoughts (e.g., on their 'frequency and contiguity'), and *not* on their contents; why then should the causal relations among thoughts respect their semantics? Why, for example, should thinking generally take the thinker *from truths to truths?* The attempt to solve this new problem by postulating a principle of association by 'similarity' was less a cure than a symptom. In fact, no associationist ever did solve it. Contemporary connectionists are still caught in the very same trap, and they have no better idea than Hume did how to get out.

The moral is: Hume saw that symbols have causal and representational properties, hence that the interaction problem is solved if there are mental symbols. What he didn't see was that the causal and representational properties of mental symbols have somehow to be *coordinated* if the coherence of mental life is to be accounted for. So, first the representation problem replaced the interaction problem, and then the coordination problem replaced the representation problem. And there the matter stood as long as mental representations were supposed to be associated pictures. So much for the last two hundred years or so.

I like Hume's story that mental representations—symbols in the head—are the locus of world-behavior interactions. But the version I prefer is that representation is information and that the mental processes that are the proximal causes of behavior are computations rather than associations. According to this revised story, mental representations can mediate the world's effects upon behavior because *the same properties of mental representations that determine their computational roles also carry information about the world.* More particularly, computation is by definition syntactic, and information is by definition etiological, and mental representations can mediate between behavior and the world because their syntactic structure carries information about their (actual or possible) causal histories. It looks like the interaction problem may be tractable on the assumption that minds are computers that are, in appropriate ways—that is, in ways that are information engendering—causally embedded in a world of mind-independent objects.

I do think that this is the closest to solving a mind/body problem that we've ever gotten. And I guess that these days everybody understands how much it depends on rejecting the idea that mental representation is a species of resemblance. But I want to emphasize how much it also depends on not thinking of content in the way that structuralists and conceptual role semanticists have always urged us to; namely, *as arising from relations among symbols.* Supposing that thoughts have *that* kind of meaning would be no use at all for explaining how thinking integrates behavior with the world. It's thus no accident that people who pursue the intrasymbolic view of content to its bitter end so often come to believe that the world must itself be a kind of text; if meaning is a relation among symbols, then if "table" means tables, then tables must be symbols too. The old, epistemological kind of Idealists used to say: 'Only an idea can resemble an idea.' The new, semantical kind of Idealists say: 'Only a symbol can resemble a symbol.' But, as the American television star Miss Piggy once remarked, it is inadvisable to attempt to eat more than you can lift. Semantics commits suicide when it tries to swallow the world. The interaction problem is hard, but it's not *that* hard.

If you start with intuitions about representation and ask how well externalist semantic theories reconstruct them, the best you get is a sort of hung jury. Externalism has Frege problems and it has Twin problems, and it has inscrutability problems, and while it isn't obvious that these problems can't be coped with, it also isn't obvious that they can. But if you start with the question how thought can both control behavior *and make contact with the world,* a semantics that reduces content to symbol-world causation is clearly what the case cries out for. If the externalist story is true, thoughts can contact the world because representation is a species of causal relation with the world. It's precisely because semantics *isn't* part of psychology that the content of our thoughts can explain the success of our behavior.

Epistemology

Suppose that all of this is, if not actually right, at least pointed in the right direction. Then it begins to be intelligible how the structure of the world can impact upon the structure of behavior even though the proximal causes of behavior are mental and not environmental; in the head, and not in the world. But intelligible is one thing, desirable is another. You might still reasonably wonder what could possibly be the point of having behavior that's caused by representations of the world. This is, in my view, a perfectly serious question; remember that reflexologists, pragmatists, Direct Realists and Heideggerians (inter alia) have all thought that the success of behavior can be explained *without* assuming that it's caused by representations.

No doubt, they say, if you want behavior to conform to the structure of the world, then if the effects of the world on behavior are mediated at all, they had better be mediated by something that adequately represents the world; in effect, by true beliefs. But why *should* the effects of the world on behavior be mediated at all? Why not suppose that behavior is caused, not indirectly by representations of the world, but directly by the world itself? Reflexes, in particular, are perfectly suited to do this work since they are, by definition, organic gestures of which the world is the proximal cause. So suppose behavior is made of reflexes, as in point of historical fact naturalists in psychology and anti-Cartesians in philosophy have almost invariably believed it to be. Then the problem how anything could mediate between behavior and the world—the very interaction problem, after all, that mental representations were invented to solve—doesn't *need* to be solved because it doesn't need to arise.

What, in short, is the point of all this neo-Cartesian circumlocution? It's a standard complaint against mental representation theories that they first invent a Veil of Ideas to be what the mind is immediately conversant with and are then perplexed how the mind can see the world through the Veil. Perhaps the representational theory really is what Freudian theory was once unkindly said to be: itself the disease of which it purports to be the cure. I think this is an objection that deserves a reply. A good theory of mind ought to make clear *why having a mind is a good idea*.

The answer, I think, is this: Mentalism isn't gratuitous; you need it to explain rationality. Mental causation buys you behaviors that are unlike reflexes in at least three important ways: they're autonomous, they're productive and they're experimental. I want to say a little about the first two, which are familiar, and then I'll close with a rather extended discussion of the third.

Autonomy

My friend Zenon Pylyshyn once offered the following argument to show that cats are less intelligent than rocks. "Rocks," Zenon said, "at least have the sense to go away when you kick them." My cat does not think this argument actually works, and neither do I. But it does point to an illuminating relation between psychology and the particular kind of externalism that informational semantics proposes.

It's a difference between cats and rocks that the trajectories of the former are not, in general, predictable from the currently impinging environmental forces. We suppose, pretheoretically and surely correctly, that this is because, though rocks act only as they are impelled to, cats, like us, often act as they decide to. So far, so good. But how, exactly, is supposing this supposed to help? Decisions involve thought, and thoughts have to represent, and we've been saying that mental states have the representational content that they do because they have the causal relations that they do. If all of this is so, how could having a mind be what makes one's behavior spontaneous and autonomous? Mental representation can't exempt you from the causal order if, as seems plausible, it is only because they are embedded in the causal order that representations represent. Perhaps it's some such line of thought that explains why, deep down, so many psychologists think that representational theories of mind must be a cheat and that some reflexological story *must* be true about the structure of behavior.

Anyhow, the argument is specious. What a thought represents is largely independent of its *actual* causal history if the informational version of externalism is true. Thoughts of cats are thoughts *of cats* not because cats *do* cause them but because cats *would* cause them under circumstances that may be largely or entirely counterfactual. Since the informational content of a thought is, to that extent, independent of its actual etiology, you can think about cats, and your behavior can be shaped by what you think about cats, even if there aren't any cats around. Because much of your behavior is caused *mediately* by your thoughts, rather than *immediately* by the world, much of your behavior is stimulus free in a way that, by definition, merely reflexive behaviors can't be. *Die gedanken ist frei* and nuns fret not in their convent cells, just as the poets say.

Productivity

Your behavior typically outruns your experience. This is because the causation of much of your behavior is mediated; much of your behavior is caused by your thoughts and the content of your thoughts typically outruns your experience.

The content of your thoughts can outrun your experience for the same reason that your thoughts can be stimulus free: although content is a causal notion, it's *possible* rather than actual etiology that counts semantically. Roughly, according to informational semantics, to think that it is raining pigs is to have a thought that you *would* be caused to have if it *were* to rain pigs. As long as the counterfactual is in place, you can think about a rain of pigs[1] without ever having been in one.

Experimentation

The sorts of arguments I've just been endorsing are familiar from Chomsky's neo-Cartesian polemics. They're among the standard reasons for supposing both that any remotely plausible account of the cognitive sources of our behavior will presuppose a representational theory of mind, and that any remotely plausible account of mental representation will have to be heavily invested in dispositionals and coun-terfactuals. If they are right, they are part of an answer to the question why it pays for the causation of behavior to be representationally mediated rather than directly environ-mental. I think that there is a lot more that's useful to be said along these lines.

We are, it seems to me, at an obvious cognitive advan-tage, not only with respect to rocks and reflex machines, but also with respect to every other kind of creature that we have so far encountered. This is *strikingly* the case. We are patently *far* cleverer than anybody else, and that we are cries out for explanation. Only the most benighted of evolution-ary gradualists could be sanguine that the apparently radi-cal intellectual discontinuity between us and other creatures will prove to be merely quantitative. Correspondingly, a good theory of the mind might reasonably be expected to say what it is that's so exceptionally good about *our* minds; in particular, what it is about our minds that allows us, alone among all organisms, to do science. Here again, I think there is much to be learned from an account of mental representation that stresses connections between content and causation.

The basic idea is this. Imagine a kind of creature that is able not just to have thoughts that are generally true, but, in particular, to have thoughts that are generally true about the contents of its thoughts. It's part of the externalist story about content that I've been telling you that content is truth-conditional; so if you know the content of a thought, you thereby know what would make the thought true.[2] And it's also part of my story that the metaphysics of content is etio-logical, so if you know the content of a thought, you know quite a lot about what would cause you to have it. My point is that a creature that knows what would make its thoughts true and what would cause it to have them, would be in a highly advantageous epistemic position: It would be able, with premeditation, *to cause itself to have true thoughts*. In par-ticular, to construct, with malice aforethought, situations in which *it will be caused to have the thought that P if and only if the thought that P is true*.[3]

I think it's likely that we are the only creatures that can think about the contents of our thoughts; hence that we are the only creatures that are in this privileged epistemic posi-tion. If so, that would account for a lot about us that is char-acteristic of our humanity; it would explain not just why we're so clever, but also why experimentation seems to be so close to the heart of our cognitive style. I want to spell this out with some examples by way of suggesting how the theory of mind that I've been commending might blend, quite seamlessly, into what Quine would call a 'naturalized epistemology'. Philosophers who are friendly to the idea of naturalized epistemology have, thus far, hardly begun to consider what such a theory would look like if psychology proves to be (not behavioristic as Quine supposed, but) representational and computational. I think the prospects are fascinating, and I propose to conclude these lectures by saying a page or two about them.

I argued in the second lecture that the notion of a 'deferential' concept really belongs to epistemology and not to semantics, and that confusion about this has been widespread to the detriment of both fields. And I promised eventually to say something about the epistemology of expertise and related matters. The time has come to cash this note. An account of the epistemology of experimentation will be seen to follow naturally.

Let's start with a simple case of consulting an expert; let's consider what goes on when you ask someone the time. To ask someone the time is, inter alia, to compose one's mind to a certain state of receptivity. To ask Jones the time, for example, is to so dispose yourself that, all else equal, if Jones says that it is X o'clock, then you will thereupon come to believe that it is X o'clock. Indeed, it is to so dispose yourself that Jones' saying that it is X o'clock will *cause* you to believe that it is X o'clock. Moreover, it is to put yourself in this receptive condition *with premeditation*. Part of *what you had in mind* in asking Jones the time was precisely that Jones should say that it is something-or-other o'clock, and that, ceteris paribus, you should thereupon be caused to believe that it is whatever o'clock Jones says it is. (Notice, however, that the hedge is essential. Jones' saying that it is 27 o'clock on the 31st of February, 545 BC would very likely *not* cause you to believe that it is. To unfrivolously ask someone the time is thus to compose one's mind to a state of *judicious* receptivity.)

But why should you wish your mind to be in this receptive state? Presumably because you are convinced that Jones is an authority about what time it is at least to the extent that, if he says that it's X o'clock, then, in all likelihood, it is in fact X o'clock (plus or minus a bit). Jones has a watch, after all; and you don't. So probably Jones knows what the time is better, anyhow, than you do. And probably he will tell you what he knows about what the time is if you ask him nicely. All this being so, by asking Jones what the time is, you contrive to put yourself in a position where, likely enough, you will be caused to believe that it's X o'clock just in case it *is* X o'clock. Since you wanted to know what o'clock it is, that is a reasonable position for you to contrive to put yourself in.

Epistemologists often remark that there is no such thing as deciding to believe that P; and, since it's arguable that you can't be obliged to do anything that you can't decide to do, there's maybe something wrong with the initially plausible idea that you are sometimes obliged to believe that P given the state of the evidence. Well, maybe. But here's something that you *can* decide to do about what you believe: You can decide to put yourself in a situation where, depending on how things turn out, you may be caused to believe that P. And, if you're sufficiently clever, you can construct this situation that you put yourself in so that the-outcome-that-would-cause-you-to-believe-that-P will occur if and only if it is the case that P. Putting a question to someone who is compliant and in the know—as when one asks the time from someone with a watch—is one species of this kind of behavior. Putting a question to Nature is another. This latter, I think, is what it is to do an experiment. The epistemology of experimentation really is continuous with the epistemology of expertise, just as the metaphor of consulting Mother Nature suggests. That this is so is another of those philosophically interesting facts that treating conceptual deference as a *semantic* rather than an *epistemological* phenomenon is likely to lead one not to notice.

An experiment to test the hypothesis that P is an environment designed to have the property that being in it will cause the experimenter to have the belief that P if (but only if) the belief that P is true. To put it slightly otherwise: An experiment is a device that's designed to cause the state of your mind to correspond to the state of the world. What you do when you design an experiment is: You ask yourself 'what outcome would make me believe that P?' and 'what outcome would make me believe that not-P?' And then you try to set things up so that you will get the first kind of outcome if and only if P is the case and the second kind of outcome if and only if not-P is the case. Or to put it still differently: the experimenter contrives to make things happen in virtue of which his future self will be an expert with respect to whether it's the case that P; an expert, indeed, to whom his present self cannot but defer.

Every experimental design is thus, inter alia, an exercise in applied cognitive psychology; at a minimum (caveats to follow) it is an exercise in cognitive psychology applied to oneself. When you run an experiment, you use what you know about what would make you believe that P to insure that you do come to believe that P just-in-case-P. Experimental predictions are generated from the theory that's being tested, *together with* the theory of the experimental environment (cf. Duhem), *together with* a (more or less explicit) theory of the cognitive psychology of the experimenter. Correspondingly, the canonical form of an experimental prediction is always "such and such, and such and such... and that will make me believe that P."[4] 'Know thyself' Socrates said; 'or no science' he might have added.

Notice that only a creature that is pretty reliable about what would make it believe that P can pursue this sort of strategy. It would go some way towards explaining *our* being reliable about what would make *us* believe that P if, on the one hand, we are generally reliable about the contents of our thoughts and, on the other hand, the contents of our thoughts is constituted by their (actual or possible) causal histories. In experimental design, everything depends on facts like this: If the stuff is acid, that will make the litmus turn red; and if the stuff makes the litmus turn red, that will make the experimenter *think that* the stuff made the litmus turn red; and if the stuff's making the litmus turn red makes the experimenter think that the stuff made the litmus turn red, then that, together with what he knows about chemistry, will make the experimenter think that the stuff is acid. The *sine qua non* is the connection between what happens in the experimental environment and the content of the thoughts that being in the experimental environment causes the experimenter to have (the connection between the stuff making the litmus turn red and the experimenter's coming to believe that the stuff made the litmus turn red). And it is precisely this sort of causal connection between the state of the world and the contents of beliefs that the reduction of meaning to information is designed to insure.

I want to emphasize that it is not an objection to this account that, instead of asking yourself what experimental outcome would *make you believe* (cause you to believe) that P, you might instead ask yourself what experimental outcome would *convince you* that P. A good way to make it likely that you will come to believe that P just-in-case-it's-the-case-that-P, is to think of an outcome that you are convinced would transpire if and only if P; and then run an experiment and see if you get that outcome. You've designed the best experiment that you can when you're as convinced as you can be that you will get the predicted outcome just when P obtains. But, of course, if you're perfectly convinced that you would get the predicted outcome just in the case that P, then if you do get that outcome, then that will cause you to believe that P. (Unless you change your mind in the meanwhile.) To be perfectly convinced that *if O then P* is to be in a state of mind in which you would come to believe that P if something caused you to believe that O.

In fact, we're only interested in an experimental outcome that would make us believe that P where we *are* convinced that we'll only get the outcome if it's the case that P. The point of running a litmus test is to put yourself in an environment where you will come-to-have-the-belief-that-the-sample-is-an-acid iff it's the case that the sample is an acid. You're interested in the outcome where the litmus turns pink only because you're convinced that if the litmus turns pink, that means that the sample is an acid. You're convinced that if the litmus turns pink that means that the sample is an acid because you believe a theory from which it follows that if the litmus turns pink then the sample is an acid. Change the theory and that changes your estimates of which experiments are worth your while to run. If, in the extreme case, the revised theory says that running a litmus test will make you believe that the sample is an acid *whether or not* the sample is an acid, then you will presumably *avoid* running the test.

Experimental inquiry is a way of manipulating the environment in aid of managing cognition in aid of forming true beliefs. So too is consulting experts. Theories function as links in the causal chains that run from environmental outcomes to the beliefs that they cause the inquirer to have. So too do experts. So the Instrumentalists were largely right about their epistemology: Our scientific armamentarium, including not just our instruments of observation but also the theories and authorities we accept, is a machine designed so that it has, as it might be, acids on one end and true beliefs about acids on the other end. Where the Instrumentalists went wrong was in supposing that this epistemological insight somehow implies a verificationist semantics.

Informational semantics corrects their mistake: Content is *constituted* externally, by causal relations between mental symbols and the world. Often enough, internalized theories *mediate* these causal relations. (Maybe they always do; that, I suppose, is what the argument about whether observation is theory laden is an argument about.) But mediation is one thing and constitution is quite another. Verificationism made what confirms what ultimately a matter of definition. But experiments aren't worth running unless the contents of the beliefs they induce are reliably informative about how the world is. You need an *externalist* semantics to explain why the contents of beliefs should have *anything to do with* how the world is. So you need an externalist semantics to explain how the experimental strategy works.

Viewing experiments as exercises in cognitive management is a key to understanding our ability to bootstrap our science. Because we have a lot of beliefs that are by and large true, including, importantly, lots of true beliefs about the content of our thoughts, and lots of true beliefs about what outcomes would be convincing that P, we are able to design environments in which we will be caused to have still more beliefs that are by and large also true. To recognize the phenomenon of cognitive management is thus to understand what is, surely, the most egregious feature of our epistemic situation: the fact that our science is (pace Tom Kuhn) largely cumulative and progressive. Given that we have a start, cognitive management predicts the acceler-

ating development of our empirical knowledge. It's not at all clear to me why one would predict this on any other epistemological picture.

I said that an experimental design is, inter alia, an exercise in applied cognitive psychology. I could have said in applied cognitive *social* psychology. Experiments are designed with an audience in mind, and I suppose it almost never happens that the only audience the experimenter has in mind is himself. To design a convincing experiment—and unconvincing ones are no use—you have to know not just what outcome would make *you* believe that P, but also what outcome would move your peers. Since the causal route from the experimental outcome to the fixation of beliefs about the experimental hypothesis is typically theory mediated, only people who believe the theory on which the experimental design is predicated are likely to be caused by the outcome to believe that P *even if the outcome does mean that P*. It doesn't, however, begin to follow that experiments can only preach to the converted; or that our science is in some ontologically invidious sense merely a 'social construct'. To be in the audience for an experiment, you have to believe what the experimenter believes about what the outcome would *mean*. But that doesn't require that you believe what the experimenter believes about what the outcome will *be*. How things turn out in experiments is up to the world. That's why how things turn out in experiments can choose among theories.

Well, enough about experiments. I use them as my main example of managed cognition because I think that, here as elsewhere, scientific methodology is cognitive psychology writ large. Experimentation is an occasional and more or less self-conscious exercise in what informal thinking does all the time without thinking about it. Cognitive management—putting oneself in a position where one will be

caused to believe that P just in case it's the case that P—is a pervasive feature of cognitive activity. You find it not just in our intentional behavior, but also in our reflexes; and not just in us but also throughout quite a lot of the animal kingdom. If there are noises off, many organisms will orient reflexively to foveate the noise source. (And if a light goes on at the edge of the visual field, the human eye moves reflexively to foveate the light.) In effect, the orienting reflex is designed to so position a creature that if (to borrow an example of Winnie The Pooh's) it was a Heffalump that made the noise, then the creature will come (and promptly too) to *believe* that it was a Heffalump that made the noise. The creature achieves this by turning so that if it was a Heffalump that made the noise, then a foveated retinal image as of a Heffalump will be formed. And the reason *that* works is that, on the one hand, the world is so constructed that almost nothing but a Heffalump ever does cause a retinally foveated image as of a Heffalump; and, on the other hand, the minds of these animals are so constructed that, if an image as-of-a-Heffalump is foveated on their retinas, then, ceteris paribus, a Heffalump belief is thereby caused in them.

It's instructive to contrast this arrangement with the famous, but apocryphal, ethology of the ostrich which, according to the story, would *rather not know* if there's a Heffalump, and which buries its head in the sand to avoid finding out. Or consider Piglet: "'It's the Heffalump!' thought Piglet nervously. . . . But he didn't look round because if you look round and see a Very Fierce Heffalump looking down at you, sometimes you forget what you were going to say." Piglet and the ostrich prefer to manage themselves out of believing that P, even if it is, in fact, the case that P, when it's being the case that P doesn't bear thinking

about. One sympathizes with their point of view, of course, but it's probably not viable outside fiction.

The moral, anyhow, is that the epistemology of the orienting reflex is unlike the epistemology of experimental design, or the epistemology of deferential concepts only in that the former illustrates cognitive management by Mother Nature rather than cognitive *self*-management. The orienting reflex is one of the little tricks that Mother N. employs to insure that, in a variety of ecologically salient cases, organisms will be caused to believe that P by happenings that mean that P is true.

But although such techniques of cognitive management would appear to be built in over a wide spectrum of the phylogenetic continuum (no doubt all the vertebrates have them), it is, perhaps, the characteristic achievement of *our* species that we have made cognitive management a project. Managing one's cognition is something that one often does literally with premeditation. That we have the kinds of minds that can do this constrains, perhaps to uniqueness, an acceptable theory of what our minds are like. My story is that premeditated cognitive management is possible if knowing the content of one's thoughts would tell you what would make them true and what would cause you to have them. The theory of mind I've been trying to sell you satisfies both those conditions. If you know that the content of your thought is that it's raining, then you know that your thought is true iff it's raining and you know that its being the case that it's raining would cause you to have the thought that it's raining in appropriately information-engendering circumstances. Off hand, I can't think of any other kind of theory of mind that would have these epistemological consequences. It is, to repeat, when you put the representational cum informational story about psychology to work in the theory of knowledge that it really starts to look convincing.

In the philosophy of mind—as, indeed, in more important matters—this has been a less than fully satisfactory century. We pretty much wasted the first half, so it seems to me, in a neurotic and obsessive preoccupation with refuting Cartesian skepticism about other minds. In the event, it didn't matter that the skeptics weren't refuted since there turned out not to be any. The only philosophers who really *were* doubtful about the existence of other minds were relentless *anti*-Cartesians like Wittgenstein, Dewey, Ryle, Quine and Rorty, and they were equally doubtful about the existence of their own. What we got for our efforts was mostly decades of behaviorism and the persistent bad habit of trying to run epistemological or semantic arguments for metaphysical conclusions. The end of this, I fear, is still not with us.

But although I try to be as pessimistic as the facts allow, I think that this fiasco really is less than the whole story. There are, increasingly, signs of an emerging naturalist consensus that is Realist in ontology and epistemology, externalist in semantics, and computationalist in cognitive psychology. And what's especially nice about this new naturalism is how much it allows us to retain of our traditional understanding of ourselves as largely rational creatures.

It used to seem that the price of a scientific world view was going to be a pugnacious denial of the importance of minds in human affairs. Science thought long and hard and announced, having done so, that thinking has no place in the natural order. (Or, if science didn't, philosophers of mind announced it on science's behalf, which was almost as bad.) You had to be very credulous indeed to be prepared to swallow that. If Positivists found it bracingly tough-minded, it struck nearly everybody else as crude, implausible, inhuman and, worst of all, irrelevant to their concerns. As Mr. Micawber might have put it: 'If *that's* what science says, Sir, then science is an ass.' No wonder if the deconstruction of scientific realism became a matter of priority in philosophy departments from the University of Paris to Emerson Hall and on to Berkeley.

As I say, I doubt we've seen the end of this, but I think that perhaps the very worst may now be over. One can begin to imagine a psychology of cognition that, at a minimum, doesn't imply its own impossibility. The productivity, spontaneity and rational coherence of behavior, which most naturalists in psychology used to feel called upon to denigrate (and which, for all the worn-out reasons, connectionists still do feel called upon to denigrate), are not embarrassments for the kind of cognitive theory that I've been endorsing. Indeed, *they're the main evidence for thinking that it may be true.* A little guarded optimism may therefore be in order as a closing note: Naturalism might turn out to be more of a humanism than, until quite recently, anyone had dared to hope. With any sort of luck, *next* century could be, as the Florentines say, 'less bad'.

Appendix A
Names

Names raise two sorts of problems for the theory that I've been trying on. One is linguistic, and everybody who is a Realist about meaning has to face it. The other is metaphysical and proprietary. They are: 'What do names mean?' and 'How shall we understand the type/token relation for names in Mentalese?'. I'll discuss these issues in reverse order.

Metaphysics: Mentalese Types and Tokens

According to me, the concept WATER and the concept H_2O have the same content; they both express a property that can be equally correctly specified as *being water, being H_2O* (or, for that matter, as *being Granny's favorite drink* assuming that Granny is on the wagon). Well, but surely these concepts are distinct, so surely something must distinguish them. What does so, according to me, is their syntax. Though tokenings of the concepts carry the same information, still the conditions for having the concepts are different: You can have WATER, but not H_2O, without having the concept H[YDROGEN]. This is because a concept is a linguistic expression (of Mentalese), linguistic expressions have their constituent structure essentially, and the concept H is a syntactic constituent of the concept H_2O. OK so far.

Consider, however, Mentalese names. I haven't, as you must have guessed, got a full-blown informational semantics for names; but it is, prima facie, implausible that if I had it would distinguish coreferring names by their meanings. For example, CICERO and TULLY both carry information about an individual who may, with equal propriety, be referred to either as Cicero or as Tully. It's not strictly mandatory (see below), but it is concessive and plausible, to assume that CICERO and TULLY carry the same information. If so, then an informational semantics cannot distinguish them by their contents.

But it can't distinguish them by their syntax either since, plausibly, CICERO and TULLY are both syntactically primitive in Mentalese, just as 'Cicero' and 'Tully' are in English. English copes with the syntactic indiscernability of these expressions by distinguishing their tokens according to their acoustic (and/or orthographic) shapes. And so too, mutatis mutandis, do the artificial languages that logicians and computers use. But, of course, Mentalese expressions don't have phonologies or orthographies, so Mentalese can't distinguish CICERO tokens from TULLY tokens in either of those ways. So, what now?

It should be clear that, although this problem arises for the metaphysics of Mentalese names, it can do so equally for any of the primitive, syntactically simple expressions of Mentalese on the (surely not implausible) assumption that such expressions can be coreferential. For this reason, I won't even consider proposals that depend on assuming that CICERO and TULLY are actually syntactically complex in Mentalese (e.g., that they are descriptions). Whether or not names are primitive, *some* expressions of Mentalese must be, and the present problem will arise for them, whichever they are.

First blush, this may all strike you as not much of a worry. To be sure, Mentalese tokens don't have acoustic or orthographic shapes. But presumably they have plenty of other nonintentional, nonsyntactic properties; neurological ones, as it might be. So long as that is so, it's OK for CICERO tokens and TULLY tokens to be identical in their meaning and syntax even though token thoughts that Cicero is Cicero are type distinct from token thoughts that Cicero is Tully.

Here's a parallel line of thought: It is central to a computational psychology that the effects of semantic identities and differences on mental processes must always be mediated by 'local' properties of mental representations, hence by their nonsemantic properties assuming that semantics is externalist. (See the discussion of the 'formality constraint' in Fodor 1980 and after.) If it is not the orthographic or phonological shapes of Mentalese expressions that play this mediating role, what is it that tokens of the type CICERO have in common in virtue of which their effects on mental processing are ipso facto different from tokens of the type TULLY? Here again, it seems natural to suggest that *any* physicalistically specifiable property will do as long as it is a physicalistically specifiable property to which the nervous system can respond selectively. Here again, homogeneity under some or other neurological description would be the obvious candidate. So then, first blush, what's the problem?

The second blush is, however, less good. If the typing of syntactically primitive Mentalese expressions requires their homogeneity under neurological description, then it would seem that at least a limited 'type physicalism' *follows from* the Representational Theory of Mind.[1] But that can't be right; it's an *empirical* issue whether, or to what extent, the type-identity thesis is true, and it's one which RTM ought to leave open at least in principle. In particular, the *coherence* of the type/token distinction for Mentalese oughtn't to rest on the *truth* of the type-identity theory. So something appears to have gone wrong.[2]

Third blush, however, everything is all right again if one is indeed scrupulous about distinguishing issues of coherence from issues of truth. Certainly, RTM should not rely on neurological assumptions to say what the type/token relation *consists in.* But it's perfectly OK for it to do so when it specifies the empirical setup by which that relation is implemented in people's heads. It's roughly the difference between explaining what relation *aboveness* is—that's a metaphysical project and must not depend on assumptions about the physics of materials—and explaining how the fourth floor of a building manages to achieve and maintain the *aboveness* relation with respect to the third floor. *That* project constrains the physics of materials all right.

I'll spare you the details, but here's a sketch of how I think it goes. The characterization of the type/token relation for Mentalese is functional, recursive, and (what else?) highly counterfactual.

Suppose we have a machine that computes in Mentalese. For convenience, suppose it has an input tape and an output tape, and that Mentalese can be written on either. I assume that we can recognize the *numerical* identity of the machine's tape states,[3] hence that the notion of *numerically identical tape states* is available to us to use for the characterization of *type* identity for Mentalese symbols.

Suppose that T1 and T2 are token inscriptions that do or can appear on the machine's tapes. Then:

1. T1 and T2 are tokens of the same type if, for any machine process (i.e., for any operation compatible with the machine's table), the numerically same output state that was (or would have been) produced by the machine when it is given T1 as input would have been produced if the input had been T2; and vice versa.

2. If Ti and Tj belong to the same symbol type by criterion 1, then Tm and Tn belong to the same symbol type if any machine process that yielded (or would have yielded) Ti as output given Tm as input would have issued in Tj as output if the input had been Tn.

3. The type/token relation for primitive expressions is closed under 1 and 2.

The basic idea is that two tokens are of the very same type if they would both cause the machine to be in the very same states; i.e., in the *numerically* same states.

So much for the metaphysical story. If one now thinks about how one would set things up so that a pair of Mentalese tokens might actually satisfy this functionally defined relation of co-typehood, it's very plausible that there would have to be some (perhaps very disjunctive) neurological description that both would be required to satisfy. Exactly analogously, it's very plausible that there must be some story about steel and concrete that explains what keeps the fourth floor above the third. That, in both cases, is how God made the world, and so be it. It no more follows that postulating Mentalese commits one to a crypto-neurological notion of type/token, than that postulating apartment houses commits one to a crypto-ferro-concrete notion of above.

Linguistics: What Names Mean

What does 'Cicero' mean? And, while you're at it, does it mean the same as 'Tully'? This is a problem in the lexical semantic of English, so if you believe in semantics you have to face it whether or not you believe in Mentalese.

To begin with, if what's wanted is a definition, I'm pretty sure you're not going to get it. Like, in my view, practically all other morphosyntactically primitive linguistic expressions, names have no definitions. About the best you can do in lexical semantics is: 'chair' means *chair*, 'cat' means *cat*, and, likewise, 'Cicero' means *Cicero*. If these platitudes strike you as unsatisfactory, perhaps you should stop asking the questions of which they are the answers.

Informational semantics may well have to say that 'Cicero' and 'Tully' carry the same information, hence that they have the same content, hence that they mean the same. So, it's true both that 'Cicero' means *Tully* and that 'Tully' means *Cicero*. It also follows that 'Cicero was Cicero' and 'Cicero was Tully' are both analytic (though, of course, the second isn't knowable a priori). What doesn't follow, however, is that tokenings of 'Cicero is Cicero' and of 'Cicero is Tully' are typically used to make the same statement. I suppose that what statement an expression is typically used to make depends on what thought it is typically used to express. And, whereas 'Cicero is Cicero' is used to express the thought CICERO IS CICERO, 'Cicero is Tully' is used to express the thought CICERO IS TULLY. These thoughts, though presumably identical in content, are nevertheless distinct. Why? Well, because one but not the other contains as a constituent a token of the concept type TULLY, and thoughts, since they are expressions of Mentalese, have their constituents essentially.

That's all, really. But I do want to stress the difference between this view and (what I'll call) the Metalinguistic View, viz., that 'Cicero', but not 'Tully', means something like *is called 'Cicero'*.

As Kripke points out, the Metalinguistic View gets the counterfactuals wrong; being Cicero doesn't require being so called. But the Metalinguistic View gets some things right too, and these shouldn't be slighted. We can, for example, learn something metalinguistic from 'Cicero was Cicero', viz., that Cicero was called 'Cicero'. What appear to be straightforwardly object-language identity claims thus warrant what appear to be straightforwardly metalinguistic inferences. But that they do so, introductions wouldn't work. I say 'This is Jones' and that warrants your inference that this is *called* Jones. 'This is this' will *not* serve to introduce Jones; not even if Jones is what both the tokens of 'this' denote.

Consider, moreover, Quine's famous example, 'so-called' (as in 'Georgioni was so-called on account of his size'); and also the deplorable telejargon 'aka' (as in 'Mary Ann Cross, aka 'George Eliot''). What, one might wonder, is the 'also' doing in 'aka'? Calling Mary Ann Cross 'Mary Ann Cross' doesn't seem to *say* that her name was 'Mary Ann Cross'; it doesn't seem to *say* anything linguistic (or metalinguistic) at all. But the inference does seem to be invited, and the use of 'aka' is intelligible only because it is routinely drawn. The Metalinguistic View accounts for all of this. There must be *something* right about it.

Although 'Cicero' doesn't mean *is called Cicero,* tokenings of 'Cicero' invite a sort of linguistic ascent in virtue of which they can be informative in ways that tokenings of 'Tully' can't. (And vice versa, of course.) 'Cicero' and 'Tully' mean the same, but my uttering the one tells you something different from my uttering the other. This is, however, pragmatics, not semantics; it has nothing in particular to do with 'Cicero', 'Tully' and 'Mary Ann Cross' being *names*.

'Poor Jones went up in a puff; he didn't know that being inflammable and being flammable are the same thing.' This explanation is both informative and intelligible (contrast ' . . . he didn't know that being flammable and being flammable are the same thing' which is neither). And yet, on second thought, how *can* it be informative and intelligible? 'Flammable' and 'inflammable' are *synonyms*. To say that being flammable is being inflammable is thus to say no more than that being flammable is being flammable. Is the story, then, that Jones died of a truth of logic?

Of course it's not. What the explanation intends, and what's understood when we grasp the explanation, is something metalinguistic. What it must have been that Jones didn't know was what 'inflammable' means. Well, anybody could get *that* wrong; from the looks of it, 'inflammable' ought to work like 'inadmissible' and 'inadvertent'. Not knowing that it doesn't might well have gotten Jones in trouble. Lamentable, of course, but no particular puzzle. The point is that here, as in 'This is Smith' or 'Cicero is Tully', linguistic ascent is invited and performed. Surely, however, the right conclusion would *not* be that 'inflammable' means *burns and is called 'inflammable'*. The right conclusion is that the story about linguistic ascent belongs to pragmatics, not to semantics.

Well, but if inviting linguistic ascent isn't particularly a feature of names, why is it so often names that linguistic ascent is invited with respect to? Why isn't 'this is a rose' used to invite the inference that this is called "a rose"? The answer, of course, is that it is; specifically, in ostensive definition. The difference is just that (barring children, foreigners and the like) one can generally rely on members of one's language community to know what roses are called; whereas even paid-up members need not know what Sam is called. So, we use 'this is Sam' to invite linguistic ascent in the normal course of business but 'this is a rose' to do so only from time to time. That we do so has misled occasional philosophers to suppose that there is something particularly metalinguistic about 'Sam' even though there is patently nothing particularly metalinguistic about 'a rose'.

Oh, well.

Appendix B
Meaning and History

According to the currently received philosophical view, thought experiments about Twins show that the actual causal history of a mental state contributes essentially to determining its content. My thoughts are about water, but my Twin's thoughts are about XYZ. This is the consequence of corresponding differences in our biographies; my causal history connects me to H_2O, his connects him to the other stuff. Similar considerations are supposed to show that my thinking about Aristotle depends on a (no doubt tortuous) causal chain that links me to him.

If all of this is right, it's an embarrassment (not for externalism per se of course, but) for informational approaches to the metaphysics of content. According to informational semantics, content depends on nomic relations among properties; to a zeroth approximation, 'water' means water in my mouth because *being water* and *being disposed to cause my 'water' tokenings* are nomically connected properties of water. Presumably such nomic connections could be in place even if none of my 'water' tokens have ever *actually* had water as its cause. Presumably, indeed, they could be in place even if there had never been any 'water' tokens, or any water. Where nomic relations are the issue, *actual* history drops out and what counts is only the counterfactuals.

Such considerations have sometimes lead even good friends of informational semantics to contemplate 'mixed' metaphysical theories according to which content is a hybrid of both dispositional and historical factors. (See, for example, Fodor 1991b.) This, however, is unaesthetic, and it looses one of the nicest features of informational semantics, its ability to provide for what I called in lecture 4 the autonomy and productivity of content. Bother Twins!

In fact, however, the evidence for historical determinants of the metaphysics of content is extremely equivocal. So, anyhow, I'm about to argue.

Consider the case of Donald Davidson's 'Swampman'. "Suppose lightning strikes a dead tree in a swamp; I am standing nearby. My body is reduced to its elements, while entirely by coincidence (and out of different molecules) the tree is turned into my physical replica. The Swampman . . . seems to recognize my friends and appears to return their greetings in English. It moves into my house and seems to write articles on radical interpretation. No one can tell the difference . . ." Still, as Davidson remarks, there's a difference there to tell. According to the historical view of content, Swampman—at least at the moment of his creation, and, presumably, for some indeterminate time thereafter—has *no intentional states at all*. No beliefs, no desires, no knowledge of anything, no views on radical interpretation. This is because he lacks, by assumption, the history of causal connections to the world on which intentional content depends.

Davidson is prepared cheerfully to accept these consequences of his semantical views. "My replica can't recognize my friends; it can't re-cognize anything since it never cognized anything in the first place. It can't know my friends' names (though of course it seems to), it can't remember my house. . . . Indeed, I don't see how my replica can be said to mean anything by the sounds it makes, nor to have any thoughts" (1987, pp. 443–444). One might, like Davidson, treat these consequences of the historical account of content as bullets that one's intuitions must learn to bite.[1] But I think they should be viewed rather as serious embarrassments for Davidson's causal history kind of externalist semantics. Of course, not having had one, Swampman doesn't remember his twelfth birthday party; 'remember' is factive, and you can't remember what didn't happen. But it seems very odd to say that Swampman doesn't know what time or day of the week it is, since (to put it in a way that of course begs the question) if you ask him what time or day it is, he is perfectly able to tell you.

If it's not his believing that it's Wednesday that explains why the Swampman says 'It's Wednesday' when you ask him, what on earth does? By this or *any* test that a psychologist could devise, indeed, by this or any test that *God* could devise, the evidence that Swampman thinks and desires, sees and hears, hopes, itches and lusts, is not different in kind or inferior in quantity from the evidence that you and I and Davidson do. To put the point another way: Perhaps it's true, as it were, by definition that beliefs, desires, lusts and the like are constituted by their histories; in which case, of course, Swampman doesn't have them. But, so what? It's intuitively plausible that he has states that are their exact ahistorical counterparts *and that these states are intentional.*

Scissor cuts paper, Swampman eats Twins. The intuitive support for a historical component in content seems not so unequivocal after all.

I think the unbiased intuition is that Swampman thinks all sorts of things that Davidson does: that it's Wednesday, and that radical interpretation is possible, and that water is wet, for example. I think this is because, although he lacks Davidson's causal history, Swampman shares Davidson's dispositions, and it's the *counterfactuals* that count for content, just as informational theories claim. True, no 'water' token of Swampman's has ever been caused by water. But Swampman means *water* by 'water' for all that. The reason he does is that it's water that *would* cause his 'water' tokens in the worlds that are closest to the one that Swampman actually lives in. Roughly, a thought means what *would* cause it to be tokened in nearby possible worlds.

A way to see the intuitive plausibility of this suggestion is to compound the thought experiments: imagine that Swampman has a Twin. Life is full of coincidences; suppose that, just at the very moment that Davidson got replaced by Swampman here, a bit of Twin-Earth got transmuted into Swampman$_2$. I think the uninstructed intuition is that when Swampman$_2$ thinks or utters 'water', *he is thinking or talking about XYZ*. I hope you share this intuition since it's the one that the counterfactual story I've been telling you predicts.[2]

But, clearly, if S2's words and thoughts are about XYZ, that's *not* because he is causally connected to the stuff since, by assumption, he isn't. Rather it's because it's XYZ that *would* cause his 'water' tokens in all the worlds that are nearest to Twin-Earth, there being, again by assumption, no H$_2$O on any of them. Similarly, S2 has thoughts (not about Aristotle but) about Aristotle$_2$. This is because, in all the worlds nearest to him, the interactions which *would* cause his 'Aristotle' tokens would trace back, via the ambient language community, to Aristotle$_2$.

Correspondingly, what makes 'Aristotle' mean *Aristotle* in my mouth is a nomic relation between certain of Aristotle's properties; viz., between his property of *being Aristotle* and his property of *being (tenselessly) disposed to cause 'Aristotle' tokens in me.* The cultural tradition that connects me to Aristotle provides the mechanism that mediates this relation, much as experts provide the mechanism that mediates the relation between *being an elm* and *being a cause of elm thoughts in me;* much as theories and telescopes mediate the relation between *being a star* and *being a cause of star thoughts in me.* The significance of cultural traditions, experts, theories, telescopes and other such mediating mechanisms is that they sustain the counterfactuals upon which the metaphysics of content depends. It is, however, their *availability* to sustain these counterfactuals, and not the actual history of their operation, that the metaphysics of content cares about.

I suspect, in fact, that it is only demonstrative thoughts whose content is determined by their *actual* etiology. Everywhere else, Twins included, it's the counterfactuals that count.

Notes

Lecture 1

1. Well, the second most important. The *really* most important thing we know about minds is that their states are often conscious. About this, here as elsewhere, I maintain a gloomy silence. Whereof there is nothing to be said. . . .

2. The notion of multiple realization belongs to metaphysics, and the notion of functional definition belongs to semantics (and/or the philosophy of science), and it is perfectly possible to believe in one but not the other. I am myself inclined to doubt that there are functional definitions because I am inclined to doubt that there are *any* definitions (hardly). But I do think that many of the properties that figure in special science laws, and probably most of the properties that figure in psychological laws, are multiply realized; specifically that they are *not* constituted by microstructural 'hidden essences'.

Not distinguishing the case for multiple realization from the case for functional definition has, I think, often lead to overestimating the importance of the latter both in the philosophy of psychology and in the philosophy of science at large. Some of Devitt's 1993 discussion in "A Defense of Meaning Localism" provides a case in point; as does some of Fodor's discussion in *Psychological Explanation* (1968).

3. Notice that this is true for Cummins whether the higher-level property is reduced or multiply realized. In the former case, it is

identified by its microstructure, in the latter case it is functionally defined. If the multiple realization of psychological states is assumed, the present problem is to understand how a creature's having a property that is computationally (hence locally) constituted could be a sufficient condition for its being in a state that is functionally defined by its *external* relations.

4. Thus, it used to be argued in defense of the psycho-physical identity thesis that it *solves the problem of mind/body interaction by not allowing the problem to arise;* if mental states just *are* brain states, the question how they are *correlated* with brain states disappears.

5. This sort of situation is not without precedent in the philosophy of mind. It's often argued, rightly in my view, that discovering the laws of brain/qualia correlation would not, in and of itself, solve the mind/body problem about consciousness. Barring an explanation of why the correlation is the way that it is, such laws would be surds; and only basic laws are allowed to be surds. (See Levine 1993.)

6. Twin cases are embarrassments for broad content psychology only if the intuitive plausibility of claiming that my Twin and I have the same intentional psychology is granted. I propose to grant it for the sake of the argument.

Lecture 2

1. The caveat is to rule out really crazy worlds that preserve our chemistry and our computational psychology but change more or less everything else, e.g., worlds where all the creatures computationally like us are brains in vats.

2. J. J. C. Smart (1962) got this right a long while back: ". . . even a color-blind person can reasonably assert that something is red, though of course he needs to use another human being, not just himself, as his 'color meter'" (172).

3. More precisely, the strength of your preference for A over B should equal the strength of your conviction that you would prefer A to B if all the facts were in. Offered a bet on a fair coin, you shouldn't prefer heads to tails; and you shouldn't think it more

likely that you *would* prefer heads to tails if you knew which way the coin will land.

4. For one example among many, see Fodor 1980, where this sort of argument is pushed very hard. Ah well!

5. However, see Fodor 1978; Salmon 1986; Crimmins 1992 and others. I'm afraid that the sort of view I'm about to expound can no longer claim to be eccentric. Drat!

Lecture 3

1. I owe a special debt to Professor Gary Gates for making me see that the putative inscrutability of reference is a more serious problem for informational semantics than I had supposed. I was slow to learn, but he persevered.

Some of the ideas that my treatment depends on were anticipated in Gareth Evans' 1975 paper "Identity and Predication." I hope he would approve of how I've worked them out. Anyhow, this chapter is a sort of *homage* to Evans.

2. Frege cases involving names raise special problems; see appendix A.

3. Unsurprisingly, time slices work in much the same way as undetached spatial parts. Suppose, for reductio, a deviant ontology according to which 'rabbit' means *time slice of a rabbit* and 'rabbit's ear' means *time slice of a rabbit's ear*. Notice that, in the normal course, a rabbit and its ears are contemporaries, so a time slice that includes the one generally also includes the other. But 'rabbit' and 'rabbit's ear', unlike 'time slice of a rabbit' and 'time slice of a rabbit's ear', are mutually exclusive. So the deviant ontology fails.

4. Well, *almost* duck soup. What the argument really shows is that either 'triangle' doesn't mean *triangle part* or 'square' doesn't mean *square part* or both. You need further argument to show that Ling ought to pick the third disjunct. As things stand, it's still open that Inf means *square* by 'square' but *triangle part* by 'triangle' or vice versa.

But here, I think, simplicity can legitimately be invoked. Barring evidence to the contrary, one ought to prefer a theory that attributes an ontology of things or an ontology of parts to one that attributes both. This is because, ceteris paribus, the best theory is one which posits the fewest kinds of things compatible with the data. This holds in the special case where the data are Inf's behaviors and the theory's posits are Inf's ontological commitments.

5. This surely can't be literally true; in linguistics there are *always* caveats and exceptions. All our present purposes require is that it's close enough to true to ground a rational presumption: viz., that if, pretty generally, Inf accepts inferences from "A is such and such" and "A is so and so" to "A is such and such and so and so," then "A" is unambiguous for Inf. If that presumption *is* rational, then there are grounds for choosing between Ling1's ontology and Ling2's, the inscrutability thesis to the contrary notwithstanding.

For what it's worth, all the systematic counterexamples that I've heard so far involve sentences with demonstratives. Thus, Elizabeth Spelke suggests that 'this is a square and a triangle' can be OK if 'is' means something like 'contains' or 'shows' (as in: 'this is a ketch and a sloop' said of a sailing print). In similar spirit, Brendan Gillan points out that 'those are squares and triangles' can be true if some of them are triangles and some of them are squares and all of them are one or the other.

Accordingly, the test for referential ambiguity I'm proposing won't work if determining which expressions of L are demonstratives requires previously determining what the expressions of L refer to. But I know of no reason to suppose that it does. That an expression is demonstrative presumably shows up in the truth *values* of tokens of the formulas that contain it (specifically, in the ways that truth values shift as a function of the context of utterance). And facts about truth values are supposed to be unequivocal for purposes of the present discussion.

6. Patently, this account assumes that Inf is *not* prepared to infer the conclusions he holds true from *arbitrary* premises; viz., that his inferential practice is not reconstructed by the truth functional '➤'.

7. I remind the reader that all this talk of knowing and needing to know is mere façon de parler. The intended claim is that the semantics of sentence (and predicate) conjunction is *metaphysically constituted* by facts about which inferences L-speakers are disposed to draw.

8. It may be useful to repeat that CN is, by stipulation, a relation among (actual and possible) *tokens* of expressions. Thus, for example, (i) is to be read as requiring that Inf is prepared to infer a token of the sentence-conjoined type whenever he is prepared to accept a corresponding token of the '*' type . . . etc.

9. Hence, of course, any property metaphysically or conceptually identical to rabbithood.

Lecture 4

1. It's widely (but, I think, erroneously) supposed that this feature of informational semantics is jeopardized by the standard intuitions about Twins. See appendix B.

2. Lepore and Loewer (1987) have argued that this knowledge must be, as it were, substantive; in particular, that if knowing a natural language is knowing a truth theory, then knowing a truth theory for L can't just be knowing that its sentences satisfy the disquotational schema "'S' is true in L iff and only if S." The crux of their argument is that someone who knows only that disquotation holds would not be able to infer from what people utter in L to the corresponding facts about the nonlinguistic world. (E.g., from the fact that people keep producing tokens of 'it's raining' to the likelihood that it's raining.)

For reasons that are beside the present point, I'm disinclined to grant Lepore and Loewer the antecedent of their hypothetical; I don't think that knowing a natural language is plausibly identified with (or even that it requires) knowing a truth definition. But I do think that the spirit of their argument is right. In effect, what follows extends it to include one's epistemic relation to the truth-conditional content of one's own thoughts.

3. The biconditional is, in fact, much stronger than is plausible and also much stronger than the case I want to make requires. For example, ". . . will be caused to have the thought that P iff the probability that P is nonnegligibly higher than the probability that not P" would do. There are deep and important issues about when it is, and when it's not, worth the cost of causing oneself to believe

that P. Clearly, it often pays to do so even though the probability that P will be true if you are caused to believe it is a lot less than 1.

But it simplifies the exposition not to worry about that here.

4. Compare the Empiricist/Positivist analysis, according to which the canonical form of an experimental prediction is always ". . . and that will make it seem to me that . . . " Notoriously, the vocabulary of seeming isn't rich enough to express the data base of science. But the vocabulary of believing must be; it's a truism that the data we have are among the things that we believe.

Appendix A

1. Type physicalism is, roughly, the doctrine that psychological kinds are identical to neurological kinds.

2. I think I first heard this sort of argument floated by Janet Levin about twenty-five years ago.

3. Including, N.B., *trans*world numerical identities at least across nearby worlds. This is the price that my story pays for access to the counterfactuals it requires. (A less extravagant metaphysics might well do for my purposes; for example, a metaphysics of counterparts. I guess I don't care much either way.)

Appendix B

1. I'm not meaning to pick on Davidson; much larger bullets are routinely swallowed whole. Thus, I've heard Ruth Millikan claim that it's sufficient to make Swampman's head contentless that he lacks an evolutionary history.

2. Entry to this game is, or course, restricted to informants whose intuitions about the original Swampman differ from Davidson's; viz., to informants whose intuition it is that $Swampman_1$ *does* have intentional states. (Anybody who thinks that $Swampman_1$ doesn't but $Swampman_2$ does is well advised to have his intuitions seen to.)

References

Crimmins, M. (1992) *Talk about Beliefs*. Cambridge, MA: MIT Press.

Cummins, R. (1983) *The Nature of Psychological Explanation*. Cambridge, MA: MIT Press.

Davidson, D. (1987) "Knowing One's Own Mind," in *Proceedings and Addresses of the American Philosophical Association*, pp. 441–458.

Devitt, M. (1993) "A Defense of Meaning Localism." University of Maryland. Manuscript.

Dretske, F. (1981) *Knowledge and the Flow of Information*. Cambridge, MA: MIT Press.

Evans, G. (1975) "Identity and predication," *Journal of Philosophy*, 72, 343–363.

Fodor, J. (1968) *Psychological Explanation*. New York: Random House.

Fodor, J. (1975) *The Language of Thought*. New York: Crowell.

Fodor, J. (1978) "Propositional Attitudes," *The Monist*, 61 (4), 501–523.

Fodor, J. (1980) "Methodological Solipsism Considered as a Research Strategy in Cognitive Science," *Behavioral and Brain Sciences*, 3, 63–109.

Fodor, J. (1991a) "The Dogma That Didn't Bark, a Fragment of a Naturalized Epistemology," *Mind*, 100, 201–220.

Fodor, J. (1991b) *A Theory of Content And Other Essays*. Cambridge, MA: MIT Press.

Fodor J. (1991c) "A Modal Argument for Narrow Content," *Journal of Philosophy*, 88, 5–26.

Fodor J. (1992) "Substitution Arguments and the Individuation of Beliefs," in *A Theory of Content and Other Essays*. Cambridge, MA: MIT Press.

Fodor, J., and Lepore, E. (1992) *Holism, A Shopper's Guide*. Oxford: Blackwell.

Lepore, E., and Loewer, B. (1987) "Dual Aspect Semantics," in Lepore, E. (ed.), *New Directions in Semantics*. London: Academic Press.

Levine, J. (1993) "On Leaving Out What It's Like," in Davies, M., and Humphreys G. (eds.), *Consciousness: Psychological and Philosophical Essays*. Oxford: Blackwell.

Putnam, H. (1975) "The meaning of 'meaning'," in K. Gunderson (ed.), *Language, Mind and Knowledge*, Minnesota Studies in the Philosophy of Science, 7. Minneapolis: University of Michigan Press.

Salmon, N. (1986) *Frege's Puzzle*. Cambridge, MA: MIT Press.

Schiffer, S. (1991) "Ceteris paribus laws," *Mind*, C (1), 1–17.

Smart, J. J. C. (1962) "Sensations and Brain Processes," (in Rosenthal, D. (ed.), *The Nature of Mind*. Oxford: Oxford University Press, 1991).

Stich, S. (1983) *From Folk Psychology to Cognitive Science: The Case against Belief*. Cambridge, MA: MIT Press

Name Index